Memories with the Trees

Memories with the Trees

A Compilation of Stories from the Appalachian and Pacific Crest Trails

Matthew J. Kline

Images: (Front Cover) – View of Franconia Ridge from Mt. Lafayette
looking towards Mt. Lincoln (New Hampshire)
(Back Cover) – Posing for a selfie on the side of Black Butte
with Mt. Shasta in the background (California)

DEDICATION

To those who believe in their dreams and have the
courage to follow them every day

&

To the Appalachian Trail Class of 2018 and the Pacific
Crest Trail Class of 2019, some of the funniest and
funkiest people I ever met in my life.

ABOUT THE AUTHOR

atthew Kline wasn't always the avid outdoorsman he is today. He had little backpacking experience except for the day hikes he did. He grew up with a love of the outdoors (especially forestry) in Western Pennsylvania just outside of Pittsburgh. After graduating from Central Valley High School, he attended Seton Hill University where he played four years of collegiate basketball and studied chemistry. After four years, he graduated with a Bachelor of Science degree in 2018.

A week after graduation, he set out to hike an 1100-mile section of the Appalachian Trail (AT). A few weeks after summiting Mount Katahdin, he started graduate school at the University of Maine. After finishing his first year of graduate school, he set out to hike a section of the Pacific Crest Trail (PCT). The trail conditions proved tougher than he imagined, and he was forced to make an early departure. He is currently a PhD candidate in the chemical engineering program at the University of Maine.

When he isn't working in the laboratory designing and synthesizing supported nickel hydrocracking catalysts, he enjoys spending time playing basketball and exploring the vast Maine wilderness. He is unsure when he will be able to complete the southern half of the Appalachian Trail, but he knows he wants to finish the trail and officially join the "2000-miler" club.

ACKNOWLEDGMENTS

Hiking a long-distance trail was no small feat. It took months of planning and preparation to be in a position where I felt comfortable hitting the trail. I could write a list that went on and on including all the people I should be thanking, but I tried to keep this section as brief as possible. From the bottom of my heart, I want to thank everyone that I was and wasn't able to list here. Without your help and support, I would never have been able to achieve my lifelong dream of hiking the Appalachian and Pacific Crest Trails!

- **To my parents:** Thank you for your unconditional love and continual support you provided on both journeys. I wouldn't have even made it out of Pennsylvania had it not been for you guys encouraging me to take the trail one day at a time. You raised me with a strong work ethic, which paid dividends for me on the trail.

- **To my siblings:** Thank you for making me laugh when I was down and for providing me with words of encouragement. You guys helped make my trip a special one, and I also should thank you guys for dealing with everything that needed to be done when I was out hiking.

- **To my friends:** Thank you for checking in on me and putting up with the copious number of pictures I sent you. Although you guys weren't out hiking with me, it felt like you were there with me every step of the way.

- **To Dr. Wheeler:** Thank you for allowing me to take months off work to spend time hiking. I needed these summer hiking sessions to recharge my batteries and to think about new directions to take my research.

- **To all my trail angels:** Thank you for all your random acts of kindness. You don't even know how big of a difference your advice and help were to the success of my hikes! You were there for me at the highest and lowest points of my trek, and for that I can't thank you enough!

INTRODUCTION

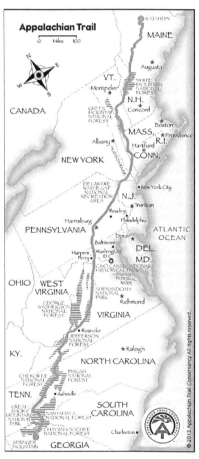

A map of the Appalachian Trail, courtesy of the Appalachian Trail Conservancy.

The Appalachian Trail (AT) is a 2200-mile footpath stretching from Springer Mountain in Georgia all the way through fourteen states to the northern terminus at Mount Katahdin in Maine. The rugged trail is the longest hiking-only trail in the entire world.

The trail was idealized by Benton MacKaye in 1921, and after more than a decade of work, the trail was completed in 1937. Slowly, the National Park Service and Appalachian Trail Conservancy partnered to purchase the land the trail crosses, and now the trail corridor is more than 99% protected.

Although an estimated two million visitors hike a portion of the Appalachian Trail each year, there are only about 6,000 hikers that attempt to hike the entire trail in a single year, a thru hike. Of those, only about 1,000 make it to Katahdin. Most thru hikers begin their hikes in Georgia in the spring and reach Katahdin by the fall, but there are also hikers that hike southbound from Maine starting in June and finish in Georgia in early winter.

The first map shows the path the trail follows across the eastern United States. The section that I hiked was from the Maryland/Pennsylvania border northwards to the northern terminus atop Mount Katahdin. This 1100+ mile stretch of trail crossed eight states and countless different towns. Along the way, I met countless trail mates and saw the vast terrain in the Mid-Atlantic and interior Northeast.

On the other hand, the Pacific Crest Trail (PCT) is a 2650-mile trail comprised entirely of three states, California, Oregon, and Washington. More than half of the trail resides in California and the southern terminus is at the Mexican border near Campo. The northern terminus is at the Canadian border, but most hikers continue northward into Manning Park, British Columbia.

The Pacific Crest Trail is a wilderness trail. It was given national status as a National Scenic Trail in 1968. The Pacific Crest Trail Association (PCTA) is the nongovernmental agency that coordinates trail maintenance and oversees future development of the trail.

Use of the Pacific Crest Trail is much more sporadic and limited. To hike certain sections of the trail, hikers need to obtain a special permit from the PCTA, which can be difficult to obtain. In certain locations in the High Sierra, the number of yearly permits is limited to protect the fragile and pristine environment.

A map of the Pacific Crest Trail, courtesy of the San Bernardino Sun.

In addition to possessing a longer length than the Appalachian Trail, the Pacific Crest Trail also passes through much rougher terrain. The first 700 miles of the trail pass through desert regions in southern California when the trail suddenly climbs to the high snow-capped peaks of the Sierra Nevadas. In the northern section, hikers must also climb through the Cascade Range to reach the Canadian border before the fall snowfall begins.

TABLE OF CONTENTS

My Prior Wilderness Experience

If you took a survey of hikers and asked them how much camping, hiking, or backpacking experience they had, more than 90% of the people would say they had too much to count. But that wasn't the case for me; camping and backpacking were foreign to me. I had hiked plenty of times before, but I only went out on short day hikes.

When I was younger, my parents took my siblings and I off on several multi-week adventures to visit national parks in the western United States. I credit them for my love of nature, and although I was young at the time, I enjoyed seeing how beautiful the western parks were and I saw how different the terrain was from the eastern states, where I had lived my entire life. In my free time, I loved being outside and hiking, but my trips to the woods always occurred during the day. Even on those long vacations, our family hiked all day, then checked in to a hotel for the night. I spent one night camping outside, but I was much younger and our tent was set up right next to our house, so we weren't exactly in the wilderness. So yes, you could say I wasn't all that prepared for life on the Appalachian Trail.

In preparation for the big hike, I planned to spend a few days hiking the Laurel Highlands Hiking Trail, a 70-mile trail across Laurel Ridge in southwestern Pennsylvania. I rode to the trailhead and hiked to the shelter that first night. It was eerie, and because it was early May, the leaves weren't out on the trees yet. I was also ill-equipped, and I didn't have a rope with me to hang my food from a tree, so I stuffed it all inside a garbage bag, climbed about ten feet up a tree, and stuffed my food in a hollow as the sun set.

I didn't sleep much that night, I kept thinking I heard movement outside. At daybreak, I walked over to and climbed up the tree I stashed my food in, but I didn't find anything there. Confused, I tried to remember if I moved my food during the night, but I was confident I didn't touch it. As my stomach rumbled, I looked around for signs of my food when I stumbled upon a shred of the garbage bag. I followed the trail of pieces down to a stream, and there I saw my food (or what was left of it). A bear must have come that night, climbed the tree, grabbed my bag, and carried it to the stream. The bear surely had a good feast, and it ate almost everything, but I noticed it didn't eat my gummy worms. However, it devoured every single gummy bear I had, so I guess it must have been a cannibalistic bear. Distraught, I sent out a distress call to my friends because I was out of food, and they picked me up less than 24 hours after I hiked into the woods. All in all, my first backpacking experience was a complete crash and burn!

I don't know how I had the mental strength to decide to continue to hike the Appalachian Trail after that experience. Despite my lack of backcountry knowledge and experience, I was somehow able to survive and thrive on the trail. When I mentioned to other hikers that the Appalachian Trail was my first time camping in the backcountry, they were all shocked. I went from never camping in the wilderness to suddenly spending more than two months in the woods, which was quite the Cinderella story!

A Day on the Trail

J ust about every day on the trail started with one of the most unpleasant sounds known to mankind, an alarm. I typically set my alarm for some time between 4:30 and 6:00, but that varied depending on the weather and how difficult the following day was supposed to be. After I hit the snooze button for fifteen minutes, I begrudgingly rolled out of my sleeping bag and started the slow process of waking up. First, I packed up my sleeping bag and sleeping pad, then I ventured out to find my bear bag. After pulling it out of a tree, I opened it and grabbed something to eat for breakfast. Typically, I ate oatmeal or Pop-Tarts, and while I sat on a log at the campsite, I looked over the terrain for the coming day. After eating, I quickly stretched, packed up the remainder of my gear, and headed out onto the trail. It usually took about an hour between the time my alarm went off and when I hit the trail.

The first few hours of the morning were always the fastest, and I used the early hours as an opportunity to get ahead of schedule. That way, if anything came up, I could coast through the afternoon or perhaps hike further than expected. About two hours into the day, I started getting hungry again, which also coincided with my legs needing a break. I tried to time my breaks to occur when I reached a viewpoint or stream, which allowed me to bask in the sunlight and eat a granola bar, fruit snacks, and some trail mix. After resting for 20 minutes, I continued onward. Those miles don't walk themselves! The 1000-ish calories I just consumed were enough to fill me with energy for another couple of hours.

All day long, I made sure to take plenty of breaks. Because I have long legs, I hiked faster than most others, but because I took so many breaks, my pace averaged out to most hikers. I usually passed hikers, then got passed when I rested, and so forth all day long. When I hiked the Appalachian Trail, I took breaks every hour, as the sheer weight of my pack caused my shoulders and hips to hurt. However, when I had a lighter baseweight on the Pacific Crest Trail, I walked for hours on end without having to stop. But I still had to stop and catch my breath when I was hiking up a mountain. Regardless of my fitness level, I was (and am) always out of shape after climbing stairs or mountains. To try to minimize the number of stops I took, I challenged myself to climb some hills or mountains without stopping on the way up. Although it was almost impossible to hike nonstop on climbs over 3000 feet, this was a good distraction on days when I had small, pesky climbs of 1000 to 1500 feet. I usually didn't make it up most times without stopping, but maybe someday in the future I also won't be panting after climbing up two flights of stairs.

By noon, I reached the midpoint of my hiking day, so I pulled out my trail guide and determined how I was doing so far. I looked ahead at my goal for the day, and I checked to see if I was on pace for that day or if I was outperforming it. Right about now, I was typically running low on water, so I filled up my water bottles at the nearest stream. On days that were extremely hot, I took an hour-long break during the hottest part of the day to help cool off. I relaxed under a tree or by a stream, and I ate more snacks and looked around at my surroundings.

While the forest may seem monotonous to some people, I always heard it bustling with activity. The wind rustled leaves in the trees, a songbird sang its melody, crickets hummed, squirrels chirped, bees buzzed by, an owl hooted off in the distance, and a stream bubbled past. It was a beautiful thing to allow the forest to speak to me; hearing all the unique sounds was something I looked forward to every day. But as I pushed northwards, the species diversity decreased, and the forests grew quieter. Regardless, there was always plenty of peace and tranquility, until I came across another hiker.

Most hikers were just like me, out in the woods to enjoy the beauty inherent in nature. However, there were some people who didn't value the peace and tranquility that came along with hiking a long-distance trail. As trivial as it sounds, hearing others talk can ruin an experience for someone else. I remember hiking in Pennsylvania near Hamburg when I was a minute or two ahead of a group of hikers. They were talking so loudly that I heard their conversation from where I was. I tried "outhiking" them, but I still heard their voices over the sound of the trees. Slowing down and letting them pass didn't work either, because they also must have stopped. I wish I told them how loud they were being, but after all, they might have reasons for being loud, so who was I to bother them?

As afternoon rolled in, the weather played a role in the remainder of my day. As daytime heating increased the atmospheric instability, I often found myself in a situation where I saw or heard thunderstorms off in the distance, which meant it was time for me to head for cover and to avoid open, exposed areas. But, if I knew the storm was moving away from me, I usually continued on. On more than one occasion, I knew I was about to take at a direct hit from a thunderstorm, so I hunkered down, pitched my tent, and hurried inside before the sheets of rains came falling down.

Around 3:30, I usually ate the remainder of my snacks for lunch. Sometimes, I ate quickly because I was in a rush to finish hiking before the sun set, or other times I started getting hungry again. By this time, the trail usually got monotonous, and unless I was in a stunning locale, I felt myself running out of steam. To combat this, I listened to music for the remaining two or three hours to power through to my destination.

When I finally arrived at the campsite or shelter (usually between 5:30 and 7:30), I was exhausted after a long day and all I wanted to do was set up my tent and fall asleep. Over my entire 1100+ mile journey, I averaged more than 16.5 miles per day, which was faster than most hikers. At that pace and with the terrain I faced, I would be in pace to hike the entire trail in about four months, one to two months less than the average thru hiker.

It was always difficult to muster the motivation to finish out the day. When I reached a shelter or campsite, my first task was reconnaissance. I had to find the best tent site to put my 2-person tent, and it was challenging (but doable) to find a suitable spot. After I selected a campsite, set down my pack, and checked how many hikers were there, I searched for a tree to hang my bear bag from. An ideal tree limb was 12 feet off the ground, 6 feet from the trunk, and the bag would be hung 6 feet below the branch it was on. Despite the months I spent backpacking, I only found two or three trees that were able to meet those requirements. Most trees in the forest were too straight and narrow to host large lateral branches, and the ones that existed were often weak and decaying. I searched for trees that could support my bag 10 feet off the ground and 3 feet from the tree trunk, but most importantly, be able to support between 10 and 20 pounds for my food sack.

After finding a bear hang location away from my campsite, I heated up water for my dinner and set my tent up. When the water started boiling, I poured it into a Knorr's pouch and stirred it multiple times. I finished setting up my sleeping bag and pad, then ate dinner. By now, the sun was about to set, so I put everything into my bear bag and hoisted it into the tree I picked out earlier. Once I marked my territory on a tree or used the privy at the campsite (depending on my mood and how far away the privy was), I zipped up my tent for the night. The next daily task I did was my journal entry. I wrote down what I saw that day and what I found intriguing, and around 10:00 I fell right asleep due to my sheer exhaustion. However, I usually was restless until midnight, and once I ensured I had no uninvited visitors (bears), I fell into a deep sleep until I heard that most dreaded sound mere hours later.

Meals on the Trail

In case you wondered what food I ate on the trail, I included a list of the food I typically ate in a single day along with the nutritional value. For breakfast, my diet usually consisted of:

Food	Calories per unit	Quantity	Total Calories	Total Fat (g)	Carbohydrates (g)	Protein (g)
Pop-Tarts	200	4 pastries	800	26	136	8
Carnation Breakfast Essentials	130	1 pack	130	1	27	5
		Total:	**930**	27	163	13

For lunch, I typically ate:

Food	Calories per unit	Quantity	Total Calories	Total Fat (g)	Carbohydrates (g)	Protein (g)
Granola Bar	180	3 bars	540	27	57	15
Welch's Fruit Snacks	80	3 packs	240	0	60	0
Trail Mix (Variety)	140	3 cups	1,680	108	192	36
Honey Roasted Peanuts	160	8 oz	1,280	104	56	56
Peanut Butter	210	6 tbsp	630	51	18	24
Little Debbie Fruit Pie	420	1 pie	420	21	47	3
Various Dried Fruit	100	1/2 package	275	0	72	3
		Total:	**5,065**	311	502	137

And my dinner usually consisted of:

Food	Calories per unit	Quantity	Total Calories	Total Fat (g)	Carbohydrates (g)	Protein (g)
Knorr's Pasta Side	480	1 packet	480	7	86	16
Knorr's Rice Side	650	1 packet	650	4	132	15
Starkist Tuna Creations	90	1 packet	90	1	4	16
		Total:	**1,220**	12	222	47

Combining everything I ate each day, my food totals were approximately:

Meal	Total Calories	Total Fat (g)	Carbohydrates (g)	Protein (g)
Breakfast	930	27	163	13
Lunch	5,065	311	502	137
Dinner	1,220	12	222	47
Total:	**7,215**	**350**	**887**	**197**

As you can see, my diet wasn't exactly the healthiest when I was hiking. I wasn't interested in eating the healthiest foods, I just wanted lightweight foods that tasted decent and sustained me for long days. One rule of thumb I followed was that I ensured all the foods I carried were at least 100 calories per ounce. This meant they were dense enough to still have nutritional value.

Daytime Weather

As I mentioned earlier, the weather played an important role every day on the trail. Before I began my section hike, I assumed that I would be able to develop skills to read the clouds to see if storms were approaching, but since most of the Appalachian Trail was in a green tunnel (see last chapter for thru hiker lingo), there was no way I could see clouds in the sky. However, when the trail surfaced above tree line or at a viewpoint, I got a good sense of the weather in the surrounding area. Meteorology interested when I was in middle school, so I knew how to read radar and I knew to trust the extended forecast (to a certain degree).

When I stopped at Omelette Karl's tent just before climbing Mount Moosilauke (in the White Mountains), I saw the weather forecast showed good weather for the next five days, but rain supposedly on the sixth day. With that in mind, I planned my next week. I knew I would be traveling above tree line for extended periods in the White Mountains, so it was crucial that I had good weather when I crossed them. I told another hiker named Gorham I planned to get over Mount Washington by July 13th because of the rain, but he told me that I was crazy to believe the extended forecast. After all, it was only July 9th and I made my schedule using assumptions for the next five days. With that forecast in mind, I increased my pace, and by adding an extra two miles onto each day, I made it over Mount Washington by the time the rain arrived. When I was hiking in the rain on the 14th, I saw a bolt of lightning strike the ridge I was on the day before, and I thought of how lucky I was to be below tree line in Pinkham Notch.

There was usually at least once point each day where I had cell service with Verizon, and I used that opportunity to check the weather. I looked at a website called 'www.atweather.org,' which was an absolute wonder and a great asset to my hike on the Appalachian and Pacific Crest Trails. The website showed forecasts for mountain peaks, shelters, and campsites, so I was able to check the forecast for where I planned to be in a few hours or in a few days. The forecasts also included temperature differences due to elevation changes and time estimates for when rain (or snow) would arrive (both were a huge help hiking in the mountains). I don't know what I would have done without those forecasts or viewing the radar on The Weather Channel app.

The weather changed in an instant on the trail, and it was always important to be prepared for anything. During my mid-summer experience on the trail, I dealt with rain, snow, hail, and hurricane-force winds. I don't want to imagine how it felt to be a thru hiker in the March or April and get caught in a snowstorm. I was, am, and always will be a fair-weather fan, so hiking in the snow doesn't sound like a whole lot of fun, but you do you!

I never could have imagined the amount of snow I saw on the Pacific Crest Trail. When I traversed Mount Hood and saw snow drifts that were as tall as me (6'9"), I felt uneasy. So, you can imagine that I was freaking out when I saw drifts more than 15 feet tall in Northern California (at the end of June)! Despite the snow that was on the ground for a decent portion of my hike, I never worried about any new rain or snow falling. From the day I started the trail until the day I finished the Pacific Crest Trail, it never rained or snowed on me, and I only saw storm clouds off in the distance once. Because I spent multiple weeks out west without rain, I understood why fires have become so prevalent in California and Oregon.

Should I Make a Campfire or Not?

Speaking of fire, people always ask me if I made a campfire every night on the trail. No. All in all, I probably had five or six campfires over the entirety of my 68 days on the AT, and most of them were during my first week on the trail. Building a fire (and keeping it going) took a lot of work. Picture yourself getting up at sunrise, walking all day, and now after trekking for 18 miles, you just made it to a campsite before sundown. Now, before you were able to start the fire, you had to make dinner, set up your campsite, and select a bear bag tree. After all of those were done, then you could go searching in the woods for dead branches and kindling to burn to light the fire. Now it probably makes much more sense at how difficult it was to find the time and energy to build a fire. But I had those fires in my first week on the trail because I had extra energy from hiking shorter days, which meant I had extra time to have a campfire.

During that time, I hiked with a group of trail mates that encouraged me to make fires. They also called me by another trail name. My trail name on the Appalachian Trail was "The Lorax," but they called me "The Fireman". I got this nickname because I hiked slower than Pacemaker, Beachbum, and several other hikers in the group, so by the time I arrived at the campsite, they had their campsites set up for the night. They were always in the process of trying to light the fire, but for whatever reason, they couldn't ever get it to light. Then, when I arrived, I set my pack down at a campsite, and one minute later, I lit the fire. I told them I was skilled at starting the fire because of I was a chemist, but the real reason was because I knew the importance of lighting dry material and blowing a finite amount of air (oxygen) into the fire. I learned these from years of experience having firepits with our neighbors in our backyard. Perhaps another question I should have asked them was, 'If I was great at starting fires, why was I called Fireman? Don't firemen put out fires?' Interesting food for thought.

On the Pacific Crest Trail, I never had any campfires. Because it didn't rain the entire time I was hiking, I knew that the area was in a dry spell and as the summer continued (without rain), the dry spell would only worsen. Eventually, all the brush dried up and died, creating perfect fire conditions. To make matters worse, days in the mountains were especially dangerous, because the gusty winds constantly changed directions. There was a Red Flag warning when I was in Northern California, meaning that 'critical fire weather conditions are occurring now due to a combination of strong winds, low humidity, and warm temperatures.' There were special rules that I was legally obligated to follow in a Red Flag Warning, and one stipulation was that there couldn't be any ignition sources for fires. This meant that I wasn't allowed to turn on my stove to make dinner every night, but I still did so, being extremely careful and cognizant of my surroundings.

Trail Conditions

Hikers tend to notice problems when they are faced with them. For instance, if a storm washed out a bridge, a hiker wouldn't know the bridge was missing until they reached the spot where the bridge was. The same goes for other trail issues, and for that reason, it was important to be up to date with current trail conditions. I originally planned to start my section hike at Harper's Ferry, but when I found out that the bridge over the Potomac River was closed due to flooding, I knew I had to alter my starting location. Luckily, I checked the Appalachian Trail Conservancy (ATC) website before I left (which said the bridge was closed), so I didn't drive to Harper's Ferry only to discover that the bridge was out. The website lists major issues that were occurring in each state, which was important for a hiker, who has no idea what lies ahead on the trail. Whether a severe weather outbreak downed a forest, or flooding rains washed out part of the trail, the website updates were useful to help hikers avoid difficult situations.

There was no universal source for trail conditions on the Pacific Crest Trail, so any news had to be spread from hiker to hiker. And although there weren't many hikers on the trail, news still spread pretty quickly. If I came upon a dangerous situation, I always tried to do my part to alert other hikers about the upcoming danger, so that they could be prepared for what lay ahead.

Keeping My Head in the Game

Keeping sane was of the utmost importance when hiking any long-distance trail. For the first two or three weeks, the trail was a physical challenge, but once I developed my trail legs, it became much easier to hike. From then on, the biggest challenge I faced was keeping my mind in the right place to finish the hike. It might sound trivial, but keeping sane was pretty hard to do at times on the trail.

I listened to music, which kept me focused on days when the trail seemed to drag on forever. I downloaded my songs on Spotify onto my phone, so when I needed a mental break and to listen to some music, all I did was I put in my earbuds and hummed away. The music helped me hike faster and it put fresh thoughts into my mind. But it also made me unaware of my surroundings, and when I was jamming out to my music in California, I heard the rattle of a Western Rattlesnake over the sound of music in my ears. Thankfully, I was able to jump back before anything happened, but I worried about turning a corner on the trail and running into a bear or not hearing the something rustling in the bushes nearby.

Another way I kept my mental health on the right track was I focused on one day at a time. Although it was easy and tempting to think about what lay hundred (or thousands) of miles ahead on the trail, I tried my best to focus on the here and now. Thinking on the order of months or weeks was much larger than I should have been thinking of, and I only planned and thought about the next two to three days ahead. Instead of thinking about the 800 miles to Katahdin, I thought of the 80 miles to the next trail town. This helped make the trail more achievable and lifted my spirits several times after enduring rough days on the trail.

An interesting mental health issue that I noticed while hiking was something that I call "Day After Civilization Syndrome," or DACS. This issue occurred after a hiker spent time off the trail and then returned to hiking. The first day back went smoothly, but the second day was absolutely miserable and made them ponder quitting. After I spent a day off the trail with my aunt in Scranton, I noticed this for the first time. My first day back on the trail went smoothly, but the following day was one of my worst days on the trail (and it didn't even rain!). I noticed the same trend when I hiked the PCT. After I spent two days off the trail with trail angels Geoff and Sylvie, I had an enjoyable day hiking across Hat Creek Rim, but a dismal day trekking through Burney Falls State Park. I would assume that I am not the only hiker to experience this (or something similar), but perhaps other people are affected differently.

My Pack Shakedown

Because I had no backpacking experience prior to hiking the Appalachian Trail, I wasn't really sure what all I needed or how much I was going to spend on my gear. Luckily, before I bought anything, I watched some videos on YouTube of other hikers describing the gear they carried with them and the stuff they didn't need. After I thought over the gear I wanted, I went to my nearest REI store and I talked with a store associate about my planned hike and got their recommendations on several types of gear. But most of their options that they recommended were pricey and some didn't work for a tall hiker; I wish that I would have learned more about budget-friendly options for gear to take along on a hike. Additionally, there was nobody on the trail even close to my height, so I didn't have anyone to compare gear items.

As a college student with a very limited savings account, I knew I wouldn't be able to afford the fancy, lightweight gear that most ultralight hikers have. To add to my problems, my 6'9" stature, made it much harder for me to find light gear because I each item I needed was larger than the average persons' gear. For most gear I needed, I only had one choice, because that was all that I fit in. Although I never made an official gear list for my LASH (Long-Ass Section Hike) on the Appalachian Trail, I made one with the gear I used for the Pacific Crest Trail, which can be accessed via the following link: https://lighterpack.com/r/6ykck7

The Big 4

The Big 4 is the name given to the four items that constitute a majority of weight in a hiker's pack: their tent, backpack, sleeping bag, and sleeping pad. The biggest and heaviest of these is the sleep system, typically a tent, hammock, or bivy sack. I preferred sleeping in a tent, because it helped avoid me looking like a giant hot dog when a bear strolled by at night. Additionally, I was able to easily lie down and store my gear in an enclosed area where nobody could touch it. As with all my other gear issues, my biggest problem was finding a tent that was long enough for me to fit inside.

REI only sold three tents that I fit into, and I chose the cheapest, but also heaviest tent, an REI Traverse 2. Because the tent was designed for two people to sleep inside, I had extra room to spread out some of my gear in the tent. Although my feet touched the end of the tent along with my hair, it was more comfortable than I thought it would be. That tent was a workhorse, and although I hiked with it for the whole AT, it was still in good condition when I got back home. For the PCT, I decided to switch to a slightly lighter tent than before, so I chose a Kelty Escape 2 tent. Although it still weighed in excess of four pounds, it was about eight ounces lighter than my previous tent, which shaved weight off my pack and thus helped increase my pace. I had no problems with the Kelty tent either, and I plan on using both of the tents more in the future.

Everything I carried depended on the size of my pack, so my backpack was the first piece of gear that I purchased. I knew I needed a lot of space, so I purchased a Deuter ACT Lite 65+10 pack. This pack had an internal volume of 65 liters and the detachable, upper part of the pack (the brain) held an additional 10 liters of gear. Although the pack weighed in at 3.5 pounds and held 75 liters, it was barely large enough to hold all my gear. This problem was exacerbated when I resupplied in town. I found that the more food I ate, the more space I had available in my pack. For the PCT, I went with a lighter and smaller pack, an REI Flash 45. Although it was two-thirds the size of my previous pack, I found it completely functional and I was able to fit all my gear into it or strapped to the outside of the pack.

Sleeping bags and sleeping pads are pretty similar, and for that reason, they are sometimes grouped together and called the Big 3. I used the same sleeping bag for both the AT and PCT, a Mountain Hardware Hotbed Spark 35° sleeping bag. Although the sleeping bag was well-suited for hiking from late-spring until mid-fall, I don't recommend camping with it when temperatures dip below freezing. I was able to stay warm for a few nights on the PCT when the temperatures dropped below 30°, but I would have preferred having more insulation on cold nights. Conversely, having a higher temperature sleeping bag was beneficial on warm nights, and I unzipped it and wore it like a blanket.

The last item in this group was my REI Co-op Trekker 1.75 sleeping pad. One of the biggest benefits of this pad was that it self-inflated, so I merely opened a valve, and it inflated on its own while I made dinner. Other hikers were jealous because of the size and cushion this pad offered, and they told me I "slept like a king." However, it was heavy and bulky, so I replaced it on the PCT with an Outdoorsman Lab UL pad. Although I had to inflate the pad every night, it was much lighter and folded down to the size of my fist, so I can't complain that it was less comfortable.

Hydration

Staying hydrated while hiking was more important than eating because of how much water hikers need. Typically, I drank between six and eight liters of water each day, which was equivalent to about two gallons of water. It wasn't possible for me to carry that much water with me, so I filtered water on demand from different springs and streams along the trail. Because I needed such large amounts of clean water, I wanted a water filter that was quick and effective at filtering large quantities of water. I originally took a Katadyn Hiker Pro Clear Microfilter pump-action filter on the AT, and although it did a good job for the first couple of weeks, it clogged easily and was difficult to clean. By the time I reached Vermont, the flow of filtered water had slowed from a stream to mere drips, and I spent 30 minutes leaning over a stream pumping to get a meager 2 liters of water, which meant that I lost at least an hour of hiking time during the day.

By the time I reached Rutland, I was sick and tired of wasting time using the pump-action filter, so I purchased a Sawyer Squeeze. I was thankful they were sold at a decent number of stores, so I purchased one at Walmart. I also think they are awesome, and I always recommend them to other hikers. A Sawyer Squeeze is extremely lightweight, compact, and did a good job of filtering. They also included attachments that connected to water bottles or used in-line with a hydration bladder. I was so happy with the Sawyer Squeeze on the second half of the AT that I took the same one with me on the PCT the following year. The filter also has a very long lifespan, and I believe it was advertised to be usable for filtering 10,000 gallons of water, so I will never need to replace it.

Now that you heard me ramble on about my Sawyer Squeeze, its time to find out what I stored my water in. When I started my section hike, I used a couple of Nalgene water bottles, but other hikers showed me there was a much easier storage solution, and about 100 miles into my hike, I made the switch. Instead of using the Nalgene-like water bottles, I started using Smart water bottles for storing water. These one liter bottles were the perfect size to fit on the side of my pack and they were super easy to replace, as I simply recycled them and bought a new one. I always kept three bottles with me, and they almost always contained enough water to sustain me through dry portions of the trail. Changing to Smart water bottles also lightened my baseweight, but I was still able to store the same amount of water.

Electronics

In today's day and age, electronics are everywhere, and many people are inseparable from their phones and other devices. To be honest, I spend a decent portion of my day on my iPhone 7 and MacBook Air, although I use them for my research work and catching up with friends. During my hike, my phone was my only way of communicating with the outside world, and I used it to check the weather and trail conditions ahead. I knew I would be in serious trouble without it, and for a few days in the Hundred Mile Wilderness, that fear was realized when my phone stopped working.

I carried several battery packs with me, and each night I charged my phone using the portable batteries. Suddenly, the night after I passed Monson, my phone wouldn't charge any more. I was 20 miles past town, and I knew I had another 80 miles until I reached the nearest road. My phone battery was already down to about 50%, and I knew it had to last for the remainder of the trail. I turned my phone off to conserve the battery, which was unfortunate because it meant I couldn't take any pictures on the latter half of the Hundred Mile Wilderness.

Luckily, I had already planned my "escape" from the wilderness, and I made it to the top of Katahdin and back to civilization without incident. When I got back to my house and tested my phone, I found that the charging cable was faulty. The electronic leads on the cable were worn down, which meant that the batteries couldn't transfer power into my phone and charge it. I could have been in an even worse situation on the Pacific Crest Trail because I relied on an electronic trail guide, but I was never in that situation.

When night came, I used an Energizer headlamp on the AT, but I hated wearing it because it produced a minimal amount of light and I could barely see the ground in front of me when I was night hiking. Before setting out on the PCT, I bought a Black Diamond Spot headlamp. I was much happier with it, as it produced a good amount of light and could easily be brightened or dimmed. I also wore my Fitbit Charge 2 on both adventures, which I found beneficial because it tracked the number of steps, mileage, and elevation change I did every day.

Toiletries

While the extremely small list of hygienic items I carried would scare most people, it was important to know that I selected only items I needed on the trail. For instance, I never carried deodorant with me because after a day or two, I was sweating everywhere and no antiperspirant in the world could stand up to that challenge. I also didn't want to put on anything that had a scent, as my likelihood of running into a bear would skyrocket. It also would be an annoyance because each night I would've had to store those items in my bear bag. I found the most important thing I carried was toilet paper (or tp). It was important to always have it handy, because I never knew when I had the urge to go. A "greener" method of doing my business involved the use of large leaves (which I did many times), but that wasn't an option when I hiked above tree line or through an evergreen forest. After doing the dirty deed, I used hand sanitizer to clean as many germs off me as possible.

One of the biggest bear attractants is toothpaste, so I tried to brush my teeth before I reached my campsite for the night. On several occasions, I brushed my teeth along the side of the trail as other hikers passed with bewildered looks. Toothpaste was also hazardous to many aquatic organisms, so I was cautious where I spit out my toothpaste and I made sure that I diluted it. When I got stuff stuck in my teeth (which happened several times), I used a small spool of floss, which could have had other uses.

Many hikers every year develop foot fungi that is caused by keeping their feet moist and not cutting their nails. I carried nail clippers with me, which worked for their primary purpose as well as a secondary one, blister popping. If I felt a hotspot developing on my feet or I knew it already turned into a blister, I used moleskin to reduce the friction and help it heal. I carried ibuprofen (for obvious reasons), multivitamins (to replenish all the nutrients I was never going to get with my diet), and allergy pills (so I wouldn't start sneezing like crazy because of pollen in the air) with me on the trail. I also brought along a few other emergency things, such as Band-Aids and a snake bite kit, which I added to my pack after I had a run-in with a rattlesnake.

Cooking

At the end of a long day spent hiking, there were few things that sounded better than kicking my feet up and eating dinner, which made sense why I thought about dinner all day long. For dinner, I typically had Knorr's Sides, instant mashed potatoes, or Raman noodles, but I needed hot water for all my dinner foods. For that task, I used a one liter Jetboil Flash, which held enough water for two people, so when I went hiking alone or with a friend. I enjoyed using the Jetboil, as it wasn't very expensive, I used it on both hikes, and it still works.

However, one downside of the Jetboil (or just about any gas stove) was that it was sometimes difficult to ignite in windy weather. Now, I imagine this was probably an issue most stoves have, but the few times I couldn't get it to ignite were upsetting. It was convenient that the stove included a push-button ignitor, so the gas would ignite without having to worry about lighting it with a match or a lighter. For gas, I have always used Jetboil canisters, I haven't tried other fuel cartridges for fear of damaging it or making an explosion. But using one type of fuel wasn't a big issue because of how long each fuel cartridge lasted. On my whole 68-day journey on the AT (in which I heated water up every night and sometimes in the morning for breakfast), I used two cartridges, one that was 100 grams and another that was 250 grams.

After I finished eating dinner, I hung my bear bag up for the night, which used a 50-foot length of 550 paracord rope. The 550 paracord meant it was supposed to withstand 550 pounds of force before breaking. I used it on both trails and never worried about the rope breaking. Instead, I was worried about the branches breaking that held my food. I packed each of my meals into separate grocery bags, and I placed all three bags inside a large 20 liter heavy-duty bag that I got at Walmart. The bags really worked well together, and when the smaller grocery bags started getting holes in them, I simply threw them away in the next trail town and got new ones.

Clothing

Life on the trail was very different than it was at home. If I was working in my yard and it started raining outside, I could simply walk inside to get out of the rain. If I took a few steps outside to get the newspaper or the mail and I felt the frigid air, I could just head back inside to warm up. And if I was too hot after working for hours in the sun, I could cool off inside using a fan or air conditioner. There was no temperature regulation out in the woods, and I had to be prepared for all the changes that happened every day. Dressing for the weather was much more imperative on the trail than at home. I wear a t-shirt and shorts for as much of the year as I possibly can (I have even shoveled snow in shorts!), but that wasn't possible when living on the trail. Every day, I endured a continuous cycle of freezing in the morning, overheating in the early afternoon, and freezing again in the evening. With each of those temperature fluctuations, I also changed my clothing as well.

Before I started my section hike, I had no idea how important it was to select certain fabrics for clothing. I made sure my clothes were made with a hydrophobic (water-repelling) material such as polyester. If I chose to wear cotton (a water-absorbing material), I could have ended up in some trouble. Cotton does a very poor job at wicking moisture away from your skin, so when I would sweat, my body could end up overheating because the sweat couldn't evaporate from my skin or clothes fast enough. On the other side of the spectrum, if I was wet and exposed to cold or windy conditions, I could have easily caught hypothermia. Because of this, I made sure I only used materials that wicked moisture away from my skin.

On cool mornings, I woke up in my t-shirt and shorts (my base layer) and put on sweatpants and a light jacket before I stepped out of my tent. By the time I left camp and started hiking, that extra layer caused me to start sweating, so I shifted back to my base layer. I wore those all day long, but if the temperature dramatically changed, I put on my jacket and/or sweatpants until I warmed up again.

To shield my body from the rain, I carried a Frog Toggs rain jacket and pants. Although the rain jacket and pants had no ventilation (and made me sweat more), they were able to keep me drier from the rain and keep my body temperature up. I also found other uses for the rain gear. I put them on to repel mosquitoes, and I also wore them to prevent my skin from getting sunburnt on the PCT. For socks, I originally wore a pair of basketball socks to start the journey, but after they got holey, I switched to Darn Tough socks. They turned out to be a good investment, as they held up extremely well and came with a lifetime warranty. So, after I finished the AT, I sent the pair back to Darn Tough, and they gave me a new pair of socks that I used on the PCT.

A few months before I started the Appalachian Trail, I badly twisted my ankle in a basketball practice. I rehabbed it for months, and I was worried about re-twisting it while hiking in the wilderness with no help around. With that in mind, I chose to hike wearing a pair of basketball shoes. That turned out to be a huge mistake, as the shoes weren't waterproof at all, gave me little support, and caused my feet so much pain after traversing Rocksylvania.

Regardless, I stuck with that pair, and when I got home after reaching Great Barrington, I switched into a pair of hiking shoes. They were an improvement from the basketball shoes, but I found they still blistered my feet and damaged my toenails.

The issue that I had with finding shoes was that I wore size 18 shoes. With that uncommon size, there were very few shoe manufacturers that make hiking or trail-running shoes that would fit my feet. I contacted Nike, Adidas, and New Balance and the first two told me they didn't make shoes that big. But New Balance told me they had three pairs of trail runners in my size in stock, so I bought all three for my journey on the PCT. They worked out well, as they had good traction in the snow and dried pretty easily. I probably should have contacted New Balance before I started the AT, but I wasn't sure if I was going to gain any traction with long-distance hiking.

Miscellaneous

I was superstitious on the trail, and I always carried my iPhone in my right pocket and my wallet in my left one. That way, I could fulfill that superstition and I didn't have to worry about losing either while hiking. I didn't want to put them in my pack, because I was worried about them getting wet or damaged. When I was hiking, I always had trekking poles in each hand, and they turned out to be an asset with all the weight in my pack. They were great for stability and they helped me lean forward, giving me more momentum to go forward. I purchased a pair of REI Traverse trekking poles on sale for less than $40, and I used that pair to hike my entire journey on the Appalachian Trail. Most hikers went through two or three sets of poles over that same distance, but I didn't have any problems with mine until I reached Monson, ME. One of the poles froze at a specific height, and regardless of what I tried to do to fix it, I couldn't adjust the pole height again. But that wasn't a big issue as I only had 120 miles remaining on the trail. I purchased the same style of poles for the PCT, and I was pleasantly surprised by how well they worked considering the price I paid for them.

Knowing where I was and when I would reach the next towns and streams were crucial to my successful hike, and I hiked the Appalachian Trail with *The A. T. Guide*. It was the most common paperback trail guide I saw on the trail, and I found it extremely helpful as a beginner. It included detailed descriptions of waypoints, trail towns, and elevation changes. I don't understand how some people hiked long-distance trails without a guidebook, its baffling to me. There were no trail guides available for the PCT, so I used the Guthooks app on my phone. It was convenient because it included maps showing the trail location and where I was as well as comments from other hikers. So, I could read comments from other hikers about the upcoming spring or town on the app. The GPS feature was also useful when I traversed snowfields, as it mapped out where I walked, and it compared that to the location of the trail.

For me to have all these stories documented in this book, I must have had a combination of a great memory and decent note-taking skills. Both are true, and my photographic memory definitely helped, as I can still clearly remember these events I witnessed on the trail. I carried a small journal with me on each trail, and each day, I wrote a journal entry before I went to bed. For personal safety, I carried my dad's hunting knife with me on the first leg of the Appalachian Trail, but the 16-ounce weight didn't justify itself. So, I sent it home and used a whistle instead. I slept each night with the whistle wrapped around my neck in case I needed to blow it. Thankfully, I only blew it twice, both times when I felt uncomfortable because I heard a large animal right outside my tent.

Some other random gear that I carried with me was a butt cushion and a rain cover. While both were helpful on the trail, the former was a luxury item while the latter was necessary. I carried the butt cushion on the PCT, but it was convenient to sit down on rocks, snow, or dusty ground and not worry about getting my butt dirty. The rain cover helped keep my pack somewhat dry from the frequent rains on the AT. If I knew there was a day-long rain event ahead, I stored all my gear inside a garbage bag, which I used as a liner inside my pack. But when it only rained lightly, the pack cover was enough, medium rain required both (rain cover and garbage bag), and heavy downpours meant that all my gear was getting soaked regardless of how well I protected it from the rain.

Interacting with Others

O n the trail, I met all kinds of people: tall and short, skinny and fat, athletic and uncoordinated, young and old, and just about everyone in between. The diversity in age groups and backgrounds that hikers had were amazing, and it was easy to keep conversations with other hikers because there was always something that we could talk about. I also met a few international hikers, mostly from Germany, the United Kingdom, and Australia. Each of them talked about how nice it must be to be an American and have all these long-distance trails available, which weren't in their respective home countries.

One thing that all hikers on the trail endured was Mother Nature. Each hiker went through the same hardships, trudged through mud on the same rainy days, and carried a heavy pack over the same distance as me. Comradery was of the utmost importance for some hikers and as a result, there were plenty of "trail families" that formed on a hike from Georgia to Maine. Although I was never part of a family, I hiked and got along with "The Northern Horde" on my first week on the trail. They were fast hikers, and their goal was to reach to Katahdin by the end of July. I hiked with them for about a week in Pennsylvania, but ultimately, I couldn't keep up with their pace. They had fully developed their trail legs after hiking for months, but my legs weren't as fine-tuned. When I got further into my hike and I was hiking faster, I tried to catch up and reconnect with them before they reached Katahdin, but ultimately they were too far ahead. They summited just four days before me, and they reached their goal of summitting in July (they did so on the 31st).

Later in my hike, I spent some time hiking with another trail family in Massachusetts and Vermont. Ultimately, though, I ended up hiking faster than them and I left them behind when we reached Rutland. Although I was always sad when I left trail mates, there were some benefits to not joining a trail family. Both examples show reasons why I wasn't right to join either group, as I was too slow for the first group, but too fast for the other, even though I got along well with both groups. I also enjoyed spending time alone, so if I wanted to be around others, I hiked with a group, but if I wanted some time to myself, I hiked alone and at my own pace. After all, the most important thing was to HYOH (Hike Your Own Hike). Below are just a few (of the very many) stories that I had with hikers and other people that I met along the Appalachian and Pacific Crest Trails.

Peaches and Bourbon

On my second night on the AT, I decided to stealth camp just past Pine Grove Furnace State Park. I set up my campsite, made dinner, and zipped up my tent to go to bed. As the sun set, I wrote my daily journal article and a few minutes after I finished, I heard rustling outside. A minute later, a voice called out, "Anybody in there?" Slowly, I poked my head out from my tent and my headlamp illuminated a short man with gray hair and a long beard. He asked me, "Hey, you want some peaches?" and held out a plastic container filled with sliced peaches, like the ones found in a grocery store. I accepted the peaches, thanked him, told him to have a good night, and watched as he disappeared into the night. I set the peaches aside, I knew better than to eat them, right?

About fifteen minutes later, I saw a light illuminate the outside of my tent and heard leaves rustling again. I poked my head out again and to my disbelief, I saw the same guy walking towards my tent. As I clutched my dad's hunting knife in one hand, I listened as he spoke up. This time, he looked down and asked, "You want some bourbon?" and held out a silver flask. I shook my head, thanked him for the offer, then tucked back into the tent as I heard him saunter off. I didn't sleep that night, I laid there with my eyes open and waited for his flashlight to appear and to hear his footsteps approaching. At first light, I packed up as quickly as possible and looked in the direction I saw him approach from the night before. I found no traces of footprints, and the direction he came from was thickly laden with underbrush. Later that day, I asked other hikers if they had seen a man who fit my description, but nobody knew anything about it. It all seemed too surreal to happen, and I wondered if it was something I dreamed, but when I woke up and looked at the side of my tent, I saw the package of peaches....

Omelette Karl

Just before I reached the base of Mount Moosilauke, I stumbled across a tarp pavilion garnished with a "Welcome to the Whites" sign. Under it, there were about a dozen lawn chairs set up and an older gentleman named Karl talking with a couple of hikers. He greeted me the way he did with all other hikers, by handing me a big glass of ice-cold fruit punch. After I introduced myself, I made myself at home while he made me an omelet. Karl asked how many eggs he should put in my omelet and after I said four, he went ahead and cracked six eggs. When they finished cooking, he filled the omelet with ham sliced right off the bone and with fresh onions and peppers he grew at his house. He pulled the sizzling omelet off the griddle and placed it on my plate. It must have weighed two pounds, and it looked (and tasted) delicious. I tried as hard as I could to enjoy and taste the food, but I still downed it in less than five minutes.

After he finished cooking, Karl sat back and told us about his life. He retired four years ago and was bored after spending his first year at home alone. But when he helped a hitchhiker into town, he had an idea for something he wanted to do. This was his third year as a trail angel, and each year he set his tent out here and cooked a fresh meal for hikers. He was fascinated by the stories that each hiker told him, and he said he was able to remember a good portion of the hikers that stopped at his tent. He asked us to jot down our trail names so he could reminisce in the winter and read through 'The Hiker Yearbook' and think back on the hikers that he met in the past year. Before I thanked him for the omelet and set on northwards, he told us about the trail we faced ahead in the White Mountains.

Krossing the Kennebec with Kim

The Kennebec River in Maine is the most dangerous stream crossing on the entire Appalachian Trail, and it is also the only river that hikers are not supposed to ford (because several people die each year trying to ford the river). There is a dam upstream of the crossing, and it can release bursts of water at any time, taking out anyone swimming across the river. Because there was no bridge across the river and no possibility of fording the river, the only way to get across was by catching a ride with the canoe operator, who ferried hikers across the river. Unfortunately, he only ferried hikers between 9:00 AM and 3:00 PM, and I arrived at the banks of the Kennebec at 4:00 PM. The clouds looked ominous and I knew there was a thunderstorm on my heels, so I started hunkering down for the night, I set up my tent, and went to the river to filter some water.

When I was down along the shore, I saw the ground was littered with a bunch of flat, rounded stones that were perfect for skipping stones. Naturally, I started skipping stones, until I noticed someone appeared on the far side of the river and shouted across to me. With the howling winds, I couldn't make out what she said, and I watched her disappear behind some bushes. I shrugged it off and a few minutes later, she reappeared, paddling across the river in a stand-up paddleboard. When she got to my side of the river, she told me her name was Kim and she asked if I wanted a ride across. I told her that I certainly would, so I ran up into the woods, packed up my gear, and headed back to the water.

When I sat down on the back of the paddleboard, I quickly noticed two things: I had no balance whatsoever, and my weight had the potential to sink the paddleboard. To minimize these problems, I laid flat on the paddleboard with my stomach on top of my backpack. Despite distributing my weight evenly and dangling my feet in the water, the back of the paddleboard was several inches underwater. When we got halfway across, the waves really started to pick up. Although we were on a river, the winds from the incoming thunderstorm were making the choppy waves approach two feet tall. Terrified, I clung onto the paddleboard, and we slowly made our way across the swells.

To add to my fear, Kim told me that the biggest person she had ever taken across was 6'5" and weighed 200 pounds. I felt a knot in my stomach, because I knew I was much bigger than both of those (6'9" and 225 pounds). To calm both of us, I explained how I got my trail name "The Lorax" and a quick portion about the Dr. Seuss book I was named after. After what felt like an eternity (but was really three or four minutes), we reached the shore. But because there were too many large rocks on the riverbank, we had to hop off the paddleboard into knee-deep water. I hopped out first, and with all the grace in the world, I slipped on a rock and fell off the paddleboard into the water. I slowly emerged dripping from head to foot, and my gear was no different.

Kim saw how deplorable I looked and offered to let me spend the night in her guest bedroom. I accepted because I wanted to get out of the rain (which started a minute later), and because it had been weeks since I last took a shower. I slowly started to dry off inside and once the thunderstorm passed, we sat on lawn chairs along the river and talked about hiking. Kim told me she had hiked several sections of the Appalachian Trail in Maine, but wasn't sure if she should go all-in for a months-long journey or not.

I told her about my experiences on the trail and how well I was able to adjust to life on the trail despite my extremely limited background in backpacking. I told her that the most important thing to keep you going was motivation and a reason to be out hiking. We ate dinner and after hearing her son tell some of his rafting stories, I went to bed. I looked out the window and saw the rain started again and I thought of how lucky I was to be inside instead of being cramped and wet inside my tent on the other side of the Kennebec. When I woke up, it was still raining outside, and Kim made me a large breakfast while I scheduled each night for the remaining 150 miles. After I thanked her a hundred times, I set out around 12:30 in the mist and hiked for a few hours before it started pouring again.

Ronnie from Israel

Because I only spent a few weeks on the Pacific Crest Trail and I was in a remote location, I didn't meet many other hikers, and few were as interesting as Ronnie. We met by chance in the Warm Springs Indian

Reservation in Oregon, where we both camped at the same campsite along the Warm Springs River. Ronnie was a short, stout fellow in his mid 40's with balding hair and a hunchbacked appearance. When he spoke, his Israeli accent shone through, and he told me stories about his experiences hiking the Appalachian Trail and about living with his mother. I passed him earlier in the day as I flew down the trail to get out of a 14-mile waterless stretch, but Ronnie had a different idea. He only planned on hiking six miles that day, so that meant he hadn't filled up his water bottles in a day and a half. He told me that he regretted not hiking faster or looking at his trail guide, and I remembered watching him stroll into the campsite an hour ago looking like someone who just finished a 12-hour shift at a mill.

Ronnie was no stranger to going slow and taking his time while hiking. He told me he hiked almost year-round on the trail, and he could be found in the winter trudging through the snow drifts along the AT. He told me about one excursion a few years ago where he got caught in a blizzard near Mount Rogers in Virginia. He spent 14 straight days at Thomas Knob Shelter because he didn't feel comfortable venturing out into the snow. I asked how he was able survive without food and Ronnie smiled and patted his rounded stomach and told me he only ate about 1,000 calories a day, the rest he gets from burning fat. He went on to say that his mom's cooking was so delicious and that she was the person to blame for him being very overweight. He hiked the entire AT several times, and a thru-hike for him typically took 9 or 10 months, but he was out on the PCT because he had one section left to finish before he completed the entire trail (albeit in sections).

Another hiker named Cosmo arrived at the campsite later that night. She had just started hiking northbound and saw plenty of snow on the trail near Mount Jefferson. Despite hiking during the winter, Ronnie was no fan of the trudging through the snow (which probably explained why he didn't leave that shelter for 14 days). He especially loathed postholing a section of trail because his feet would get wet and he would tire out easily. He wanted, in his words, "someone with much bigger feet to walk in front of me so I don't have to make footprints in the snow as the posthole sucker." To this day, when I think of hiking through the snow, I picture Ronnie creeping behind me while snickering because I was the "Posthole Sucker."

Geoff and Sylvie

After I made the decision to bail from the Pacific Crest Trail because the snow was too dangerous, I was 26 miles from the nearest town. To get there, I had an initial 8-mile walk on unpaved National Forest Development Road 4220, and then another 18 miles on National Forest Road 46 until I reached Detroit, Oregon. When I finally made it off the first dirt road, I started walking on the side of the paved road for about ten minutes until a car pulled alongside me and the driver asked me if I wanted to hop in and get a ride. I gladly accepted, and we drove towards Detroit. Geoff was looking for Elk Lake Campsite, but when we couldn't find it, we headed to Detroit Lake, where he planned to spend the night with his dog, Sylvie.

When we reached Detroit Lake Campground, the park rangers told us that all the campsites were booked solid because it was Father's Day weekend. So, Geoff asked if I wanted to go back and crash on his couch for the night, and in the morning, I could catch a bus to California. I agreed, and after what I expected to be a short ride to his apartment, turned out to be an hour and a half ride to the Oregon state capitol, Salem. We talked about my life on and off the trail and I mentioned about the situation that I was in and that I needed to kill some time while the snow melted. He told me that he planned to go to Astoria the following day and he invited me to come along. We talked about plans for the next day while we ate authentic New York-style pizza, then we drove to the dog park. Sylvie had a blast running around and chasing after her and other dogs' tennis balls, and afterwards we went back to his apartment and watched *Mr. Woodcock*.

That night was the first time I fell asleep and felt secure since arriving on the West Coast, and I woke up feeling refreshed and excited. Geoff made pancakes and bacon for breakfast while I took Sylvie for a walk around the block to burn some of her energy. Once we ate breakfast, we drove two hours to Astoria, and got to see Lewis and Clark National Historical Park. We visited Fort Clatsop, the site where Lewis and Clark spent the winter of 1805-1806. After, we got an opportunity to see the Pacific Ocean, and we drove south on Route 101 until we decided to stop and eat an early dinner at an oceanfront restaurant in nearby Cannon Beach. It wasn't the prettiest of days, as low clouds rolled in from the ocean and the temperature was only in the upper 50's. But regardless, it was exciting for me to see the Pacific Ocean for the first time in over a decade, as I barely remembered seeing it last time.

On the way back to his apartment, I drove and got to drive a truck for the first time in my life. Once I got used to the size of the vehicle, it was much better, but I still worried if anything happened to us because it wasn't my car. We took the scenic route along the rocky shoreline of the Oregon Coast, and there we saw the hidden coves and rocky outcrops that jutted out into the Pacific Ocean.

We followed the GPS on Geoff's phone and suddenly, it told us to turn off the paved, Oregon Coast Highway onto a small, unmarked road that passed a couple of farms. I didn't question it, and I kept driving further down the road, past where the pavement ended. We ventured further and further into the mountains of the Oregon Coast Range, and the terrain got exponentially rougher. An hour later, we ended up on a bluff in the middle of nowhere, and after it seemed like we drove in circles for 30 minutes, we got out of the car and assessed where we were. Both of our phones had no reception, and the road was at a T, so we had to decide which direction to head. Unfortunately, with no reception, neither of our mapping programs worked, but when I was in a pinch a few days ago on the PCT, I downloaded an app called 'Maps.me,' which had maps of all roads and trails in Oregon. I had the maps already downloaded on my phone, and once I pulled up the map, I saw that we needed to make a right turn. Eventually, we reached the highway again and were able to make it back to his apartment in one piece.

Once we made it back, we watched *The Blues Brothers* before heading to bed. After the movie finished, I fell asleep on the couch. When I woke up to the sound of my alarm in the morning, I packed up my gear and we drove down the street to the bus station. We got there at 7:30 and once I checked in at the Greyhound station, I said goodbye to Geoff and Sylvie. I told Geoff how extremely thankful I was for him to host me for both days, plus pick me up from the trail and allow me to tag along to Astoria. As the bus pulled away, I waved them a final goodbye.

Animal Encounters

The definition that the United States sets when it designates Wilderness Areas is, "an area where the earth and community of life are untrammeled by man, where man himself is a visitor who does not remain." And while humans are only temporary visitors in these areas and everywhere in the forest, there are a great many more organisms that call that place home. Each forest ecosystem is home to a vast number of plant and animal species, and it was important while hiking to be mindful of the other species found along the trail. During the thousands of miles I hiked, I saw a decent number of others, and some interesting encounters are detailed here.

Bears, Beets, Battlestar Galactica

Of all the animals that I feared on the both my hikes, bears were at the top of the list. Although I am a very big person, I know that things would not have gone well for me if I found myself face-to-face with an angry bear. Although I saw plenty of signs of bear activity, I only had a couple of sightings and I never was in an extremely dangerous situation. If I would have had to fight a bear, that would have ended badly for one of us....

I had never seen a wild black bear before starting the Appalachian Trail. A few weeks into the trail was when I spotted my first bear in Wawayanda State Park, New Jersey. Right before I saw it, I ventured off the AT to explore some abandoned iron mines. I set my backpack down along the side of an overgrown dirt road, and I set out on foot to explore the ruins. After looking around the old mine, I turned around and headed back to my backpack when I suddenly turned a corner and spotted a baby black bear along the side of the trail. I froze in my tracks and hurriedly looked out for the mother bear when the baby bear darted off the road into the woods. I had no choice but to run past where the bear was to get back to my backpack. After seeing my pack was unscathed, I headed to the shelter a mile away and kept alert for the bears to come back.

When I left the trail for a week while I was in Massachusetts, I left my dad's hunting knife at home. With that, the only safety mechanism I had was my whistle (and if you call it a means of protecting me is questionable). My next bear encounter occurred at Kid Gore Shelter in Vermont. In 2019, the shelter was infamous for bear sightings, and the Appalachian Trail Conservancy posted warnings about the bears. I was hiking with some trail mates and we arrived at the shelter just before the sun was setting. We set up our tents spaced between two large campsites, twenty yards from each other. After I ate, set up my tent, and hung my food for the night, I said goodnight to the others and headed into my tent to write my journal entry. About 20 minutes after the sun set, I heard rustling outside my tent. I whispered to ask Zoltan (who was in the tent next to me) if he was stirring around and he said no. A minute later, I heard a bloodcurdling scream coming from Caveman. We all jumped out of our tents and went over to Caveman, who was still in shock. He didn't put up his tent fly, and when he rolled over and saw the black bear standing over his tent, he screamed. Luckily, it was such a loud scream that it scared the bear off, and after we calmed Caveman down, we all went back to our tents, but we couldn't fall asleep.

A week later, I was hiking alone on July 4th, when I reached a viewpoint of Ascutney Mountain. There I saw a field full of ripe raspberries, so naturally, I decided to eat my fair share of them. After picking for about 15 minutes, I stood up and looked at the edge of the clearing and saw an adult black bear standing on its hind legs staring at me. I paused, then let out a loud roar. It stood there unafraid until I let out an even louder scream, which caused it to turn around and run away. It was about dusk, and for some reason, I thought it would be a good idea to camp near that clearing so I could eat some more raspberries in the morning. But, when it got dark and I was laying in my tent, I heard the bear outside the tent walking in circles. I clutched my whistle and prepared to blow it, when off in the distance I heard the hiss and crackling noise of a firework. The bear took off in the ensuing firework barrage, and I fell asleep uninterrupted by my furry friends.

When I hiked the PCT, I didn't see any bears per se, but I saw plenty of signs that they were around. At almost every campsite I visited, the nearby trees had claw marks all over the tree trunks. Since I was hiking alone and in prime bear territory, I was alert all day long. That really took a toll on me, and I worried more and more about a bear attack or if a bear ate my food and I had to go days without it. On the AT, I knew there were always other hikers around, but on the PCT I had to fend for myself. I got a case of "Bearanoia," and I fell asleep every day worried that I would see and be forced to fight off a bear that night. Thankfully that never materialized, but all the worrying took a toll on my mental health and was a partial contributor to me being unable to finish my PCT hike.

I encountered another bear along the AT when I spent a weekend hiking in Shenandoah National Park with my friend Meghan. After an exhausting day of hiking, we dropped off our gear at Byrd's Nest 3 Shelter and set off down a fire road to filter water from the spring. When we reached the spring, we huddled over the piped spring with our water bags when we heard a nearby tree shake. We both looked up, and 40 feet off the ground was a black bear eating branches at the top of a tree. He spotted us, clambered down the first ten feet, and slid down the bole like a fireman. When he landed, he was merely 20 feet from us, and we froze and slowly backed away from the bear. The bear landed on the ground and reared around and darted back into the woods as we breathed a collective sigh of relief.

Oh Deer

If I had to pick one animal species that I find annoying, white-tailed deer would win that award. In most every state, they are everywhere and overabundant. While they may look cute and fuzzy, I had to remind countless day hikers that deer were still wild animals and could harm humans. Because deer are overabundant and over the carrying capacity in some locations, many are dying due to disease and starvation. One such disease is Chronic Wasting Disease (CWD), a fatal disease caused by a prion that can wipe out deer populations in North America. Though there have been numerous attempts to quarantine deer, there are still many cases of wild deer with CWD. I saw a deer with CWD when I was in Pennsylvania, and I alerted park officials in Swatara Gap State Park about the deer. However, you shouldn't worry about the world running out of deer, as they are plentiful and not going away anytime soon.

Since the time that Europeans arrived in the Americas, deer are one of the few species that have seen their population explode. Part of this is because humans eliminated many deer predators, and another reason is because deer habitat has increased. Deer need clearings to survive, and before Europeans arrived in the Americas, there was almost unbroken forest from the East Coast all the way until the Great Plains. Unfortunately, deer have also become accustomed to humans, and some actively seek out humans for food.

When I was on the PCT near Grizzly Peak in California, I came across a deer standing in the middle of the trail. As I usually do, I waited for it to move, but it stood its ground. It stared at me then started walking in my direction. I took a few steps backwards, and when it kept approaching me, I clapped my hands to warn it. The deer finally understood and sidestepped off the trail. But, as I passed it, the deer started following me down the trail. After it followed me for 50 yards, I turned around and started yelling at it, but once I threw a couple of stones in its general direction, it finally turned around and sauntered away.

Loonie Tunes

I spent the summer of 2017 in Maine, and I found that Mainers were so excited about loons. I had never head of a loon and I was confused at their excitement until I saw a loon and heard it make its call. The sight of the loon was amazing, as was its screech. In case you haven't seen a loon or can't remember what they look like, loons have bright red eyes, a black neck, and a checkerboard-like design on their backs. Given those unique features, it makes sense why they are featured on Maine license plates. When I met a hiker in Pennsylvania named Loonie Tunes who spoke all about loons, most hikers were confused, but I knew exactly what he meant. He was a Mainer and had perfected his loon call, which he displayed at each lake we passed. He knew that when he heard the loons call back to him for the first time, he was getting close to home.

I didn't see any loons on the trail until I was in Maine, and it was actually a few days before I finished the trail that I finally saw a loon. I set up my tent at Rainbow Lake Campsite and walked to the lake at dusk to filter some water. As I sat on the beach, I looked to the center of the lake and saw two loons feeding in the middle of the lake. While I watched them, a group of about five hatchlings emerged from a grassy patch to my left and headed out into deeper water to be with their parents. I heard the loons screech a minute later, and just like Loonie Tunes, I felt right at home.

Amoosing Moose Sightings

Everyone is excited to see a moose, even people here in Maine that see them all the time. The same is true for someone that has never seen a moose before. I had seen only a handful of moose in my life, and I knew I had a good chance to see one in Vermont, New Hampshire, and Maine. With that in mind, I tried to wake up early in those states if I knew there was a pond nearby so I could possibly see a moose feeding in the lake. I was disappointed after hiking in Vermont, as I saw perfect moose habitat, but there just weren't any. I assumed New Hampshire was also going to be difficult to find a moose because of the terrain in the White Mountains, so I figured my best chance to see a moose was in Maine, a state known for moose sightings.

In my time on the trail, I only ended up seeing one moose, and it was in New Hampshire, a few miles from the Maine border. I stopped for the night at Gentian Pond Campsite, and when I finished making dinner, another hiker ran up to my campsite and said there was a moose down at the pond. I assumed they it was a joke, but after hearing it was in fact real, I quietly rushed down to the edge of the water with the other campers. Lo and behold, there was a cow (female moose) on the other side of the pond wading a few feet out in the water. We all watched her for the next 30 minutes, as she went about eating dinner from the bottom of the pond. After watching the moose for a while, I realized I left my food unattended near my tent, so I ran up to get it, but by the time I returned to the pond, the moose had gone.

Even though Maine was moose-less for me, I saw plenty of moose droppings. The AT in Maine felt like I was just dodging giant piles of moose poop every hundred feet or so, and for a lot of the trail, that was a real issue. I had never seen moose poop before, so it made sense that I was very confused after seeing all these piles of about 100 bulb-sized pellets on the trail. It wasn't until I talked to other hikers that I found out they were actually moose droppings. They coated the trail and I know for a fact that despite trying my best to avoid them, I stepped on a ton of them during my hike.

Snake and Shake

Perhaps one thing that me and Indiana Jones have in common is our common fear of snakes. Although my fear wasn't developed because I fell in a crate of snakes, I am afraid of them and aware of their venomous potential. While most snakes along the Appalachian Trail were not venomous, the three snakes I was leery of were the Timber Rattlesnake, Northern Copperhead, and Eastern Massasauga, though the latter is endangered and rarely seen. One piece of information that was music to my ears was that there were no venomous snakes found on the trail north of Massachusetts. That came in handy when I was in the White Mountains and in Maine, where I did a lot of climbing on rocks, so I didn't have to worry about snakes.

My first encounter with a snake was just after Duncannon, Pennsylvania, when I came across a powerline crossing. Pennsylvania is prime habitat for snakes because snakes live in rocky areas, which are abundant throughout the state. As I walked across the path through the rocky clearing, I heard the rattle of a rattlesnake coming from the side of the trail. I screamed and ran ahead before I had the chance to find the snake.

A few days later, I had another altercation with snakes at Dan's Pulpit. I read the trail register at the viewpoint, and some SOBO hikers wrote down that they had seen rattlesnakes 100 yards north of the summit. After I hiked what I thought was 100 yards, I still saw no sign of the snakes, so I figured it was a joke or something like that. I sped up my pace and 30 seconds later, I stopped mid-step and looked down where I was about to step. As I stepped down off a boulder, there was a timber rattlesnake coiled up below my foot getting ready to strike! In shock, I leapt backwards and fell onto the ground. My eyes burst wide open when I looked first to my left, then to my right and saw all of the pit vipers that surrounded me! My heart raced, and I scrambled to my feet as quickly as I could, then I quickly surveyed the ground to find a path out of the rocky depression. I was surrounded by at least ten rattlesnakes (that I could see), and I found an area where none of them were laying at and jumped out of the bowl-shaped depression. It took me a minute to calm down and once I breathed a huge sigh of relief, I bushwhacked a quarter of a mile out of my way to get as far away from those timber rattlesnakes as possible.

That incident scarred me, and when I reached Palmerton, my aunt bought me a snakebite kit. It dawned on me how lucky I was to get out of there alive and without being bit. Had I not looked at my foot mere seconds later, I would have definitely been bitten when I stepped on the snake. Another lucky note was that none of the snakes in the pit lunged at me or attacked me as I walked in the first time. Had I been bitten, I was four miles from the nearest dirt road, and then from there, it would have been a long drive to the nearest hospital to get anti-venom. Had something happened, I would have been glad that I had cell service, as I would have been able to call 911 and call for an ambulance or speak to a snakebite expert on the phone. To survive a snakebite, the victim has less than a day to get the correct anti-venom, and exercise (like walking four miles to the nearest road) dramatically decreases the chances of survival as the bloodstream spreads the venom around more easily. I was lucky enough to get out in one piece, but I felt bad that I couldn't warn any other NOBO hikers about the snakes. I guess I hoped that they took the trail register seriously.

Given all the trouble I had with snakes on the AT, I wasn't excited to be walking through Hat Creek Rim, a desert along the PCT in northern California. I taught myself the names and varieties of rattlesnakes that inhabited the area, and I was worried about hiking out there alone. I had a smooth trip through Hat Creek Rim, but a few days later when I wasn't expecting it, I had another run-in with a rattlesnake.

Two days before I finished the Pacific Crest Trail, I crossed the McCloud River and I was blasting music in my earbuds. I passed a group of slow-moving older hikers and I was feeling good, the miles were going by quickly and the day was almost over. As I jammed out to "Mr. Blue Sky," I suddenly heard the rattle of a rattlesnake over the sound of music in my ears. I leapt backwards and saw a Pacific Rattlesnake hiding in a small patch of grass beside the trail. Normally, I would bypass this singular rattlesnake, but I couldn't because the trail was on a steep-sloped section of a mountain. My first instinct to get it to move was to throw objects at it, so I started by throwing branches. When that didn't work, I moved to something larger and started hurling rocks at it. After a couple of direct hits, the snake finally yielded and slid off the trail down the mountain. I breathed another big sigh of relief, as I knew I was even luckier that I didn't get bit now than before. At the spot where I got bit, I was fifteen miles from the nearest road, and I had to hike about ten hours in either direction on the PCT to get cell service.

Quarrel with a Squirrel

Although squirrels look cute and cuddly and I used to enjoy watching them scurry around the forest floor, my view of them is forever tainted. The squirrels that I passed in Vermont and southward were well-behaved and kind to hikers, but upon entering New Hampshire and Maine, they got rebellious. They hissed and chirped at me as I quietly walked down the trail. They stood near the edge of the trail, then scurried up a tree and catcalled at me when I passed. Despite the continual harassment I got throughout New Hampshire, everything pales in comparison to the morning after I reached Andover, Maine.

It was a typical morning; I rolled out of my sleeping bag and groggily pulled my bear bag out of a tree. Then I grabbed some Pop-Tarts and sat down on a fallen log and started eating breakfast. Out of nowhere, I felt something hit my head, but I shrugged it off, thinking it was a small branch falling from a tree. The same thing happened again, and I looked up in the tree and saw a red squirrel chucking acorns at me! Before I react, it hurled another acorn at me and hit me on my arm, so I responded in kind by throwing a rock at it. And although the squirrel scurried away and hid in the upper branches of a balsam fir tree, the other red and gray squirrels continued to harass me throughout Maine, even on my way climbing down from Katahdin. Because of my "traumatic" experience with squirrels, I am going to hate squirrels for the rest of my life.

Stories from the Trail

W hen I started hiking the Appalachian Trail, I heard some crazy stories from other hikers, and I wondered if I would have any of my own by the time I finished the trail. By the time I finished the trail, I ended up having a lot more stories than I imagined, and I tried my best to explain some of them in detail here. In this chapter, I describe some of the interesting sights that I saw along the trail and I explore in detail some of the decisions that hikers are faced with that test their resilience.

What Do They Call a Falling Tree? Timber!

"If a tree falls in a forest and no one is around to hear it, does it make a sound?" While philosophers could argue all day about this question, I never thought about the philosophical implications of the question, but instead I pondered about the mathematical odds of seeing a tree fall? I figured after hiking more than 1100 miles through almost-uninterrupted forest I was due to see a tree fall in front of me, right? I had no idea how often trees fell in a forest, so I didn't really know what to expect. I assumed that the odds of a tree dying in the summer are probably lower than in the winter, where snow and ice could wreak havoc on trees struggling to survive. Think about it, how often does anyone see a tree naturally fall over? And no, cutting a tree down doesn't count! In all the times I went hiking, I only saw branches fall off in front of me, but never an entire tree topple over.

Although I hiked on some days with gusty winds, I never saw anything but branches fall from trees until I reached Mount Greylock. It was cold, misty, and raining at the summit, and I knew a big storm was rolling in that afternoon, so I tried to hurry to the next shelter. Just as I was about to reach the spur to Wilbur Clearing Shelter, I heard a snap to my right and I whipped around. Just like that, I saw a tree about a foot in diameter snapping at its trunk. I paused for a second as it started to fall, then a look of fear spread across my face as I realized it was falling towards me. I took a few steps backwards just in time to watch the 30-foot tree come crashing to the ground. It landed a few feet from where I was standing, and I would have been hit if I didn't move backward. I set my pack down and tried to move the tree off the path, but it was too heavy to pick up, so I snapped some branches off to clear a path. Then I hurried on the spur trail to the shelter so I could get there before another tree fell near (or on) me.

I was happy that I saw the tree fall, but I was also worried because of how close it was to me. Had the tree fallen on me and trapped me, I would have been discovered because I was on a popular stretch of the trail, but had it happened in a remote location, I could have been hours or perhaps a day away from getting help. When I was hiking near Andover, Maine in a remote trail section, I got to watch another tree go down, but this time the tree fell away from me. Although I never felt the same surge of fear and adrenaline that came with the first experience, I can say that I saw two trees fall in a forest, and yes, they each made a sound!

Tent Life or Shelter Life?

One debate that hikers had was whether sleep in the shelter or in their tent (or hammock). When I started the trail, I spent most days sleeping in the shelter, as I wasn't sure how I would feel sleeping in my tent (and I was still scarred from the "Peaches and Bourbon" incident). However, after about a week on the trail, I spent a few consecutive nights in my tent and I never went back to sleeping in the shelter. On those days, I arrived late to the shelters, which were already full, so tenting was my only option. But I also fell in love with sleeping in my tent. Not only was I able to sleep without having to hear other people snoring or making noise, but I could also get up whenever I wanted to and do whatever I pleased. Additionally, my tent weighed almost five pounds, so I wanted to be able to say that carrying the tent was worthwhile.

On my first night on the trail, I slept at Birch Run Shelter. Because it was my first time in a shelter, I wondered when the other hikers would get up to start their day. Bright and early at 6:30 sharp, Hairy pulled a bugle from his pack and started playing it, much to everyone's dismay. That was an annoying wake-up call, but I didn't sleep all that much that night anyways because my nerves got the better of me. However, as I hiked for more and more hours each day, I found it easier and easier to fall asleep. There was a saying for hikers that went, "If you didn't get a good night of sleep, you didn't hike enough miles during the day."

Tenting was usually my go-to move, but I was still open to sleeping in a shelter if there was a thunderstorm coming or if there were no campsites. Most shelters had room for four or eight people, but at Wilbur Clearing Shelter (did you hear that name recently?), we managed to stick eight hikers into a shelter designed to fit five. There was a thunderstorm barreling down on us, and we all squished in and got all up in each other's space, but it was better than being out in the rain. Especially since right before I arrived at the shelter, a tree almost fell on me, so I didn't want to sleep under a widowmaker that fell on me as I slept that night. It was a better move to have all of us squeeze into the shelter to avoid taking chances.

Humans weren't the only animals that occupied the shelters. Most nights when I slept in the shelters, I woke up in the middle of the night to the sound of something scurrying around in the walls or ceiling of the shelter. Most shelters housed a thriving population of rats or mice, and some colonies were worse than others. When I reached Happy Hill Shelter in Vermont, I read that other hikers reported there was a family of pack rats that lived in the shelter and they were known to steal possessions. That night alone in the shelter, I slept with my headlight on my head, and when I heard something moving, I flipped the light on to locate the rats. One time I turned the light on and I found myself staring right into the eyes of a rat that was about to grab my phone. After shooing it away, I thought about what I would have done had the rats gotten away with any of my belongings.

I never wanted to worry about losing my stuff again, so after that night, I never spent another night in a shelter. Tent life won out, and now when I go camping and would have the choice of sleeping in a tent or a shelter, I would always choose my tent. That ended up working out in my favor, because there were no shelters along the Pacific Crest Trail. All the hikers ended up tenting or hammocking as they ventured through the Sierra Nevada and Cascade Ranges.

You Can Look, but You Can't Touch

As I wandered (stumbled was probably more appropriate) through the forest, my eyes were constantly looking down at the ground (especially if I was in Pennsylvania) or wandering through the trees. I looked for anything out of the ordinary and for animals or poisonous plants. While the poisonous plants weren't like Venus fly traps that ate or poisoned humans, poison ivy, oak, or sumac all gave nasty rashes to any hikers who touched them. I was mainly concerned about poison ivy and poison sumac on the Appalachian Trail, whereas I worried about getting poison oak on the Pacific Crest Trail.

When I was younger, I used to get poison ivy all the time. I played outside in our yard every day, and I had no idea what poison ivy looked like, which was a recipe for disaster. When I got to high school, I studied forestry for the Pennsylvania Envirothon, and I was finally able to recognize poison ivy. Now, I tell everyone what poison ivy looks like, so hopefully they can learn that they can look at poison ivy, but they just can't touch it.

After walking for days on end, it was impossible for me to ensure that I didn't step on or touch poison ivy, and I ended up getting it twice. The first time, the rash appeared on my arm and it spread up and down my arms, but the second time, I got it on my feet. The chemicals that are responsible for the allergic reaction on your skin are called urushiols. To clean them off your skin, soap and water need to be applied to the affected area to dissolve the nonpolar irritant and to wash it away. Unfortunately, soap was very dangerous to the environment, so I didn't carry any with me. The best that I did was apply hand sanitizer (isopropanol) to clean it, but even that had limited success. Although the itchiness eventually wore off, it was still difficult trying to resist the temptation of scratching my skin. I also felt bad for one hiker that I knew that used poison ivy accidentally. He was searching the forest for a "greener" alternative to toilet paper, and he accidentally ended up picking up some poison ivy and using it. He told me he was off the trail for a week because he needed medical attention and he could barely move. A doctor prescribed an antibiotic cream to him and after being bed-ridden for a week, the rashes started disappearing. I am certain he will never mistake poison ivy for another leaf ever again!

Unlike poison ivy, I had never been exposed to poison oak before, and I couldn't identify it until I was in northern California. Before I left for the PCT, I read a trail guide that mentioned that poison oak was abundant near the McCloud River, so I was aware of it when I hiked there. Sure enough, I found it everywhere, and I tried to destroy some of the plants overhanging the trail by swinging my trekking poles at them like a baseball bat. After chopping down plants left and right for an entire day, I accidentally touched the lower part of my trekking poles, which were coated with the plant urushiols. I didn't realize how big of a mistake that turned out to be.

Later that night, I went to bed and noticed my arm was itchy. I instantly regretted chopping down those plants, and I wondered getting poison oak was my karma for killing the plants. The rash started as a small patch on the side of my arm and spread like a wildfire. Even after I spent a day off the trail where I took several showers with soap and water, I couldn't get rid of the rashes, and they only spread. Even a week after first getting it, more bumps still appeared every day. Finally, two weeks later, I visually saw the number of bumps decreasing on my skin. Perhaps the rash was so bad because it was my first time contracting poison oak, but regardless, I was miserable for weeks because of it.

Challenging Myself on the Trail

As if the Appalachian Trail wasn't already difficult enough, some hikers need more challenges along the way. There were plenty of optional challenges that hikers enjoyed, and if a someone don't want to be a part of it, they didn't have to (there was very little peer pressure on the trail). As for me, I wasn't a huge fan of doing some of the challenges, or "food marathons" as I called them, because many required eating ridiculous amounts of food (like a five pound burger, three pound steak, or gallon of milk. I figured that I would probably ruin those foods for the rest of my life, which wasn't the reason I chose to hike the Appalachian Trail.

The challenges started right away for me, and on my second day on the trail, I experienced the Half Gallon Challenge. As a reward for reaching the halfway point on the Appalachian Trail, most hikers attempt the ice cream challenge, where they have 30 minutes to gorge on a half-gallon of ice cream. I went into the Pine Grove General Store and bought myself a half-gallon of moose tracks ice cream, figuring that I may as well enjoy the ice cream I ate, but I instantly regretted it. The ice cream was so rich and it sat in my stomach like a rock, and I regretted not choosing vanilla or chocolate. I tried to eat as much as I could, but I only finished about 3/4th of the ice cream. One thing that didn't help my cause was that it was 11:00, and I ate breakfast 3 hours ago, plus I didn't have hiker hunger, like most of the thru hikers had. Craft E was able to finish his half-gallon of Neapolitan ice cream, so I can say for the first (and only time) in my life, I was out-eaten by a 65-year old.

Another challenge that most hikers participate in is called the 24-hour challenge. This challenge involves hiking as far as they possibly can in a 24-hour period. Hikers typically start this challenge around 3 AM, hike for a few hours in the dark, power through the day and finish their hike at 3 the following morning. The highest mileage that I heard of in the 24-hour period was 60.3 miles. Although that number would be almost impossible to most people (including me) on the AT, such a high number like that was possible on the PCT, where the terrain was much easier and more forgiving. I planned beforehand to do the 24-hour challenge over Hat Creek Rim, the desert-like region in northern California, but the timing got all screwed up on my hike and I ended up hiking that section during the day so I never really tried the challenge. My body also preferred a steady pace, as I would rather hike two days of 20 miles than one day of 40 miles and then a day to rest.

There were plenty of other challenges that hikers chose to partake in. One of them was the Four-State Challenge, where the goal was to hike through four states in just one day. For a NOBO hiker, this meant starting in Virginia, crossing through West Virginia and Maryland, and finishing the day in Pennsylvania. Another challenge was the Pennsylvania Pizza

Challenge, where hikers ordered pizza for dinner each night while hiking through Pennsylvania. There were a good number of challenges in Pennsylvania, probably because they helped distract hikers from the horror that was the Appalachian Trail. One final challenge I will mention here was the McDouble resupply, where the challenge was only buy McDonald's McDoubles sandwiches for a resupply. With that, hikers only ate McDoubles for breakfast, lunch, and dinner until they reached the next town (which made me want to throw up when I heard about the challenge). There were also plenty of trail towns along the way that had food challenges that catered to hikers with hiker hunger.

2018 Hiking Season Weather

Like every year, there was some strange weather that occurred in the months preceding my hike on the Appalachian Trail. The first incident that affected most hikers was not a day-long situation, but rather a series of unfortunate events for hikers. The 2018 winter was particularly varied, as January and February temperatures trended well above average, but in March and April, the pattern completely reversed. There were four nor'easters alone in March 2018, which brought large snowfalls and brutally cold temperatures everywhere on the trail, including the southern portions. Almost all hikers I spoke to said that this was the worst late winter/early spring they had ever witnessed. The cold and snow also forced a record number of hikers off the trail. The ATC projected a success rate of about 28% for the year 2018, but the winter weather was a major cause for the actual success rate to only end at about 15% for the year.

The next event that some hikers faced (although it was minor) was a fire that closed a 20-mile stretch of trail in Virginia. In late April/early May, a fire broke out on Catawba Mountain, near McAfee Knob, and the multi-day blaze lit up over 150 acres. Luckily, the forest service was able to control the blaze before it grew too far out of hand. I didn't meet any hikers that were forced to stop because of the fire, but most hikers were aware of the fire and knew that the fire danger was higher in spring than in any other season. Although most news about fires tends to come between the summer and early fall months (when the Santa Anna winds create massive fires in southeastern

California) that isn't the case for the AT. On the East Coast, fires are most prevalent in the spring because of several factors: abundant fuel on the forest floor (because of dry, dead leaves from last year), no shade to block the sun from heating the leaves on the ground, and abundant thunderstorms; all of which contribute to the increased fire risk.

A few days after I graduated from Seton Hill University, there was a string of supercell thunderstorms that hit the Newburg, NY (Hudson River Valley) area. Several tornadoes touched down, but most of the damage to the area came from a large macroburst. The straight-line winds exceeded 105 mph and affected an area three miles wide by eight miles long. It just so happened that the Appalachian Trail passed right through the affected area, so the trail crews had a huge cleanup there. From the day the storm hit on May 15th until the day I got there, trail crews worked nonstop to clear the trail. When I arrived, I was greeted by a group of trail volunteers who were cutting the last of the downed trees outside the RPH Shelter. Although the trail was technically clear of downed trees, it had obvious detours and was marked with small, temporary flags as the trail winded through the downed debris.

The weather in Pittsburgh is similar to most of the surrounding Mid-Atlantic states, including West Virginia, northern Virginia, and Maryland. A few days after graduating, but before I began the Appalachian Trail, a low-pressure system stalled over the region, and many locations saw huge rainfall totals. For instance, the area around Harper's Ferry picked up six inches of rain between May 15th and 19th. With all that precipitation, the Shenandoah and Potomac Rivers were both in flood stage by the time I planned to start my hike on the 20th. Before I was about to leave for Harper's Ferry, I checked the trail conditions and found out that the Amtrak bridge over the Potomac had flooded and was closed. Additionally, the C&O Canal Towpath was flooded for three miles, and hikers who made it across the bridge before it closed were forced to trudge through shin-deep water on the towpath. Because I knew the Amtrak bridge was closed on the 19th, I had no choice but to change the starting location of my hike from Harper's Ferry 40 miles northward to Caledonia State Park.

The bridge remained closed for four days, and it was only open for about a week before it was shut down by flooding again. Another stationary front stalled over the same area between June 1st to 4th, and flooding was once again a major concern. This time, the flooding was more widespread, and some different areas of the trail flooded. Flooding struck Baltimore and the surrounding region, and I talked to hikers who waded through Rausch Gap under almost a foot of water. It just so happened that I passed through the area a few days before. But after that storm system passed, the weather remained fairly normal for the remainder of the hiker year, so there weren't any other major issues that hikers faced in the latter half of 2018 except for a slightly early arrival of winter, but that didn't bother me because I was already in graduate school at the University of Maine.

My Elusive Hiking Shoes

As I mentioned in my gear shakedown, I started hiking the Appalachian Trail with a pair of basketball shoes. And as I hiked further into Rocksylvania, I realized how big of a mistake that was, and I knew I needed new shoes that actually provided support for my feet. When I reached the Delaware Water Gap, I finally caved and looked for a pair of shoes. I couldn't find anything for size 18 hiking shoes on Nike, Adidas, or New Balance, so I decided to try a new company, bigshoes.com. This was my first time ordering shoes from them, and after I talked to a customer service representative on the phone, I asked for a pair to be shipped via USPS to the post office in Greenwood Lake, NY, where I would arrive in four days.

I never heard back from them about any shipping issues, but when I was about to reach Greenwood Lake, I saw I had a voicemail from FedEx on my phone. I thought it was strange that I had a message from FedEx when I specifically said for the shoes to be sent via USPS. The voicemail said that FedEx had my package, but they couldn't deliver it to the address I provided. I called them back, told them who I was and the situation that I was in, and asked to get the address changed to Fort Montgomery, NY. They said they couldn't do anything until they had permission from Big Shoes. So, I called Big Shoes and got a voicemail saying that their customer service center didn't open until 10 AM central daylight time (it was 9:30 EDT). I had no choice but to continue on hiking, and when I got cell service later in the day, I called the number three times, but each time, nobody picked up on their end. By then, I already passed through Greenwood Lake, where the post office workers told me they didn't have a package for me. The next day, I finally got ahold of Big Shoes and they assured me they would get the shoes redirected to the address I gave to them in Fort Montgomery.

Two days later, when I reached Fort Montgomery (by now my feet were killing me), I walked to the post office in town and asked if they had a package for me. The postal worker said there was nothing for me, so I called Big Shoes and found out that they wrote down the address I gave them incorrectly. I was at a loss for words and cried as I sat along the side of the post office parking lot. To avoid any further complications, I decided to have the shoes shipped directly to my house to avoid further complications. My plan was for my parents to mail me the shoes from my house, but as it turned out, I was home a week later for my brother's graduation party. There, I got a chance to break-in my new hiking shoes, which were less comfortable than I imagined, but they were still better than my basketball shoes. The new shoes lasted the remaining 675 miles on the AT and provided much more support for my feet, but if anyone wanted large-sized shoes, I wouldn't recommend bigshoes.com to a friend.

Looking for a Train

One of the weird goals that I had during my LASH of the Appalachian Trail was to watch a train pass in front of me. I always lived near railroads at home and at school, so when I heard or saw trains, they reminded me of home in the strange, new world I was in. The first set of train tracks I passed that looked in-use were just outside of Boiling Springs. I planned to wait by the side of the tracks for 15 minutes while I ate lunch, but when I arrived, I saw an electrical crew working by the tracks. I figured they would probably be suspicious of me waiting there. So, I walked into town, and not five minutes later, I heard a train whistle off in the distance. By the time I turned around and walked through a couple of side streets to view the crossing, the train had already passed. I crossed several more railroad crossings in the Cumberland Valley, but I waited at each one to no avail.

Disappointed, I knew my next opportunity was in Duncannon, where trains traveled up and down the Susquehanna River, so after I crossed the river, I sat on a pile of old railroad ties and rested. I didn't see a train go by, but a trucker came up to me and asked if I saw "Pee Paw" on the trail. He had been following her trek online, but I told him that I heard she was a week behind me. The next sizable railroad was in the Schuylkill Gap, and to hear my train experience there, check out the section on Hamburg/Port Clinton, PA. Long story short, I accidentally walked on a main railroad line at night, and a train approached from behind and scared the living daylights out of me. The Lehigh and Delaware Water Gaps were also quieter than I pictured.

When I hiked over Bear Mountain and into Fort Montgomery, I heard trains pass by along the Hudson River, but I wasn't able to catch a glimpse of them. I crossed the Bear Mountain Bridge and waited on the far side of the bridge, but after waiting for twenty minutes, I gave up.

I was stubbornly determined to see a train, and I knew that I would see a train at the next railroad crossing. There was only one railroad stop along the entire Appalachian Trail, and I knew it was ahead. The Metropolitan Transportation Authority (MTA) operates the ATRR station, and hikers could hop on the train there and arrive in Grand Central Station a few hours later. I reached the station fifteen minutes before the train's scheduled arrival time, so I sat on a bench at the station and patiently ate a pizza fritte. About ten minutes later I heard a train whistle in the nearby town of Pawling. Not two minutes later, the train appeared out of the forest and blared its horn as it flew by the station without stopping. I was sitting about ten feet from the tracks, and the huge gust of wind from the train almost knocked my lunch out of my hands. I finally got to see a train in broad daylight, but I was shocked at the sheer size and noise the train made. Perhaps hiking in the woods changed my size and noise perceptions?

I didn't expect to see any other trains along the remainder of the trail, because the terrain in the interior Northeast was tougher and more sparsely populated than the Mid-Atlantic states. I was partially correct, and I didn't see anything until I got into the Hundred Mile Wilderness (of all places). I forded Big Wilson Stream as the sun set, and I hurriedly set up camp above the riverbank before a thunderstorm hit.

I slept soundly until I heard a train whistle off in the distance at 12:50. I dozed off and woke up 15 minutes later when I heard the train approaching. As it got closer and closer, the sound it made got worse and worse. It made a horrible, high-pitched screeching sound as the wheels must have crossed a faulty section of track. The screech was so loud that it forced me out of my tent. I stood out in the thick fog and although I covered my ears, the sound still pierced my eardrums. After what seemed like forever (but was perhaps five minutes), the train passed, and the noise slowly faded into the night. To add to my confusion, I didn't know I was near a set of railroad tracks and a thick fog blanketed the entire forest, so I couldn't see which direction the train was coming from or going. In the morning, I found that I had camped about 100 yards from the tracks. Several other hikers stayed at the nearby Wilson Valley Lean-to also complained about hearing the train, so I was glad that I wasn't the only person who was imagining things!

After I finished hiking the Pacific Crest Trail, I decided to spend a night in Dunsmuir, California. When I reached Interstate 5, I found my only ways to get into town were to walk along the side of the interstate (which was illegal and dangerous) or to hike along the railroad tracks (which was also illegal and also dangerous). I went with the second option and as I got about a half-mile from town, I saw a train approaching. I calmly stepped off the tracks and positioned myself against the hillside to allow the train to pass. As it passed, the engine noises were so awfully loud sound. My eardrums felt like they were bursting because of the noise, and thankfully, the conductor didn't stop the train and get out to yell at me walking along the tracks.

Thinking back on the last two train experiences, I think the reason that my eardrums hurt so badly after the trains passed was because I was used to the sounds of nature, which have low sound intensities. Because I was suddenly exposed to 90 decibels of sound (after days of nonstop 40 decibels), my eardrums couldn't prepare for the loud sounds emitted by the freight trains and my felt like it was about to explode each time.

Tales of "The Lorax"

How Did I Get My Trail Name?

One of the sacred rituals on the Appalachian Trail are trail names. On the trail, almost no one goes by their real name. Instead, they go by their trail name, a unique name that they gave themselves or someone else gave to them. Most hikers fell into the latter category, and their name was derived from some unique characteristic in their personality or something they did on the trail. Although some hikers were embarrassed by their trail names, most were proud of their names, because it showed they had an alter ego, someone different than the person they showed every day.

As I mentioned several times in passing, my trail name on the Appalachian Trail was "The Lorax." I was a couple of days into my hike when I found myself sitting around a campfire with Pacemaker and Beachbum. I went on a rant about trees and all their other uses, and when Pacemaker picked up a piece of red maple (*Acer rubrum*) to burn in the fire for a slow-burning log, I scolded him. I told him to throw it off to the side and to look instead for some oak or mountain maple. When they returned with a few pieces of Northern Red Oak (*Quercus rubra*), they asked why it was better to burn the other wood. I explained how the oak burned slower and had a higher heating value than soft maple, which was the characteristic you wanted for a fire. After I told them more facts about the trees around me, Pacemaker stopped me mid-sentence and said, "Wait, there's your trail name, it's Lorax!"

I fully embraced my given hiker name, but I knew there was another hiker on the trail that year who went by "Lorax," so I decided to differentiate myself from the thru hiker by calling myself "The Lorax." As it turns out,

Lorax was famous along the trail because he wrote part of the Dr. Seuss novel *The Lorax* on a privy wall all the way back in North Carolina, and some hikers remembered him for that. I never met him, but it would have been interesting to see which one of us was more deserving of the trail name Lorax.

Keeping the Bugs Away

Bugs were everywhere along the trail, but there were a few that hikers ever cared about. Of course, the two main ones that annoyed the living daylights out of hikers were mosquitoes and black flies. They were omnipresent in the woods, but if the timing of your hike was just right, you could wind up in a much better or worse scenario than other hikers.

When I was in New Jersey hiking along Kittany Mountain, I was in the wrong spot at the wrong time. It just so happened that on that day, the black flies in the area hatched. They coated the trees and the trail, and the swarms of flies looked straight out of a horror movie. But despite their presence and the innumerate number that landed on me, they didn't understand how to bite through my skin. Another weakness was that they were also extremely slow, so I was able to kill just about every one that landed on me.

Reminiscing on that moment, I wonder if the flies and mosquitoes were so resilient later in the summer because all the weaklings were killed early on? Is it possible that each year, we might be selectively killing off the slower breeds of mosquitoes? Does that mean mosquitoes in the future are going to fly much faster and have worse bites than the ones in the past? That would be an interesting evolutionary study that might deserve an investigation.

To protect myself from the bugs, I sprayed a chemical called permethrin on my clothes. It binds to fabric and supposedly kills any flies, mosquitoes, ticks, and chiggers that land on the applied areas. I noticed a difference in the number of mosquitoes around me, but that effect only lasted for two weeks, less than the advertised six weeks. For times when the permethrin wasn't enough, I also carried a spray bottle of Off Deep Woods. That bug spray was great for getting the swarms of mosquitoes off me, and although it didn't stop them from biting me entirely, it decreased the number of bugs who attempted to bite me. And because most mosquitoes kept away from me, I was able to effectively kill most of them as they landed on my skin.

Compared to other hikers, I was a less-bitten hiker. I knew people that were constantly harassed at the same campsite I was at, but they didn't bother me. That didn't mean that I never had to worry about bites, it just meant that I ended up with a bite or two instead of five or ten. On the Appalachian Trail, the only bad states for me were in Massachusetts and Maine. There, I was constantly attacked by the mosquitoes, and even after I zipped up my tent for the night, the mosquitoes buzzed right outside my tent. One of the worst things in the morning (besides hearing my alarm) was waking up to the sound of mosquitoes buzzing outside my tent, waiting for me to start eating my breakfast so they could eat theirs too.

I thought the mosquitoes were bad when I was in Maine (and particularly the Hundred Mile Wilderness), but they turned out to be so much worse in Oregon on the PCT. When I reached a dry stretch in the Warm Springs Indian Reservation, I was harassed by mosquitoes until I reached a water source. There, they left me alone for a few minutes, and just as I bent over the water source to fill up my Sawyer Squeeze, they all swarmed me. I was coated in mosquitoes, and I found myself wildly flailing my arms around to entice some to get off. That occurred over a fifty mile stretch of the trail, but all in all, dealing with the mosquitoes and black flies was worth it for all the beauty I saw on both trails.

Living Thrifty on the Trail

Hiking the Appalachian or Pacific Crest Trail doesn't have to be an experience that breaks the bank. Before I hit the trail, I did some research on what an average thru hike cost. The results showed a wide span, from around $2,500 to more than $10,000. As a poor college student, I didn't have the kind of money to live lavishly, but I had enough to always be fed and still enjoy myself on the trail. I kept my costs low during the hike because I budgeted my trip before I left. I knew where I was going to stay, how much I planned to spend on food, and how much my gear would cost. Because of that, when I was on the trail hiking, I didn't have to worry about figuring out how much money I spent at each town, I just had to hike the trail.

Since I had no overnight hiking gear before the trip, I knew I needed to buy everything new. I didn't want to get used gear and I wasn't sure how well I would fit into everything. The reality of shopping for hiking gear is that cheaper items were heavier than the more expensive, lighter one. However, there was a point where it wasn't worth spending an extra $100 to shave an ounce or two off my baseweight. Despite having to buy all my gear new and in larger sizes (which cost more), I ended up spending about $1,000. While that might seem like a lot, most hikers I spoke to spent between $2,000 and $2,500 for all their gear. Additionally, you could imagine that amount was sort of a rent charge, since there was no fee to camp in the woods.

I was able to save more money because I knew how important timing was to my trip. I had several months to look for gear before I left for the trail, and I usually found most of the gear items that I wanted on sale. When I found the items on sale, I sprung on the them. The result was that I had gear from multiple different companies, but I was able to get savings on almost every item I needed to help keep my costs low.

The up-front costs were the single-biggest cost of hiking the trail, and the remaining costs were spread amongst the weeks and months I spent on the trail. I only spent my money on trail to buy food, but hikers could also buy rides to/from the trail, hotel/hostel rooms, and just about anything a hiker wanted. The only "required" cost needed from towns was the food for a resupply. Everything else was optional, and this was an area where other hikers had their budget run away. Hotel rooms were very expensive, even if they were split between several hiking buddies, and the cost staying at a hostel added up too. During my time on the Appalachian Trail, I didn't spend any money staying at hotels or hostels. I reckoned that since I was already out in the woods carrying my insanely heavy tent around, I may as well use it.

I also watched out for fees for staying at shelters and campsites. There were some places in the Green and White Mountains where hiker fees were used to deter the cost of maintaining facilities. I avoided staying anywhere that I knew I had to pay, which included the White Mountains, where I stealth camped every night to avoid paying the $10 campsite fee. That added up, so by spending those five nights in stealth sites, I saved $50, which was enough for about three days' worth of food.

It doesn't take a rocket scientist to keep costs at a minimum. All it took was someone who knew the value of something and what they were willing to pay for it. To keep myself honest, I always asked myself, "Do I really need this?" when I was about to buy anything. This method allowed me to cut down on a lot of the expenses that I had, and like all lessons I learned from hiking, it didn't just apply to trail life.

The Bubble

Most NOBO thru hikers begin their trek in Georgia in March (and less in February and April), and over the first couple of months, the faster hikers advance ahead of the pack, while the slower ones lag behind. This natural separation between hikers over time follows a normal distribution curve. Although the faster hikers end up in front and slower hikers end up behind, there is a giant blob of hikers in the middle, called "The Bubble."

One goal for my hike was to stay away from the bubble. There were several reasons why, and one was because it spreads hiker resources thin. Because there is a concentrated band of hikers, overcrowdedness runs rampant. Shelters and campsites fill up beyond their capacity, trail towns overflow with hikers, and the peace and solitude that so many hikers look forward to is gone.

In my opinion, it was better to be out ahead of the bubble rather than in the middle or behind. I didn't want to deal with all the hikers, so I knew I didn't want to be stuck in the bubble, but I also wanted to hike at my own pace. Although I had to hike faster to stay ahead of the bubble, I enjoyed solitude on the trail and the forest hadn't yet been trampled by the throng of hikers passing by. If I hiked behind the bubble, I knew I couldn't hike very fast, because I would end up passing through the bubble, which I didn't want to do. It is also important to note that the size of the bubble changes every year. Some years, the bubble is two weeks wide, while other years it is a month wide. The size depended on the number of obstacles hiker faced and the dates hikers decided to start their trek on.

When I hiked the Appalachian Trail, I started the trail about two weeks ahead of the bubble. I knew I didn't want to get stuck in the bubble, so I hiked faster and tried to outpace most other hikers. My strategy worked, and by the time I reached Massachusetts, I had a comfortable three week lead on the bubble. But after spending a week off the trail with my family, I had to regain the lost ground that everyone had made up on me. Since my trail legs were fully developed, I had no problems regaining the lost ground. By the time I reached Katahdin, I was about a month ahead of most hikers in "The Bubble".

Night Hiking

Night hiking is a love-hate relationship with hikers, as some hikers really enjoy it, while others despise it. I fit into the second group, and I know I would rather hike during the day and sleep at night (like normal people). For me, it was already difficult enough avoiding tripping on rocks or getting lost during the day, so I can't imagine how much worse it would have been had I hiked at night over a rocky section.

I only went night hiking once on the Appalachian Trail. After a long day, I got a hitch to the trail from Rangeley, Maine. I reached the trailhead as the sun was setting, and I knew I still had two miles before I reached Piazza Rock Lean-To for the night. At the trailhead, I met up with Coyote (or Overcomer) and we decided to tackle the night hike together. He had been night hiking plenty of other times, so it was beneficial to go with him. Hiking wasn't as difficult as I imagined until the last rays of sunlight disappeared over the horizon.

Once it was pitch black, I started tripping over the roots and rocks that littered the trail in Maine. The dense forests didn't help as well, as they shielded everything a few feet from the trail out of my view. When I heard sounds around me, I wondered if a predator, like a coyote or a bear, was approaching. However, after a long hour in the dark, the silhouette of the shelter came into view and we stumbled out of the woods and set up our tents in the dark. I wouldn't have been able to keep calm without Coyote, and for the remainder of the trail, I never contemplated trying it again.

Just as most hikers prefer hiking on sunny days, night hikers prefer hiking on nights with a full moon. In the spring especially (because the leaves aren't on the trees yet), the moonlight penetrates down onto the forest floor, and hikers can look around and see a decent amount of the forest. Although it is much darker than how it looks like during the day, once your eyes adjust to the light, hikers could still make out shapes and objects. It was cloudy out when I went night hiking, so I had no light other than my headlamp illuminating the trail in front of me. But that didn't stop some people from night hiking, as they didn't have preferences about the moon phases. But overall, most night hikers preferred the full moon hike, and every month when the moon was full, a group of hikers hiked all night long. They asked me several times if I wanted to go, but I turned them down every time, until I had no choice but to go night hiking with Coyote.

Furry Friends on the Trail

Although it may seem difficult for some people to believe, there were plenty of hikers who thru hiked the Appalachian Trail with their canine companions. I grew up with dogs and was always around them, but I would never put them through the strain of hiking the AT. But that didn't stop some people from bringing their beloved furry friends on the walk of a lifetime!

There are reasons that you shouldn't bring your pet along on the trail (and yes, I saw someone with a cat on a leash hiking the trail). I imagine that walking all that distance can't be good for your dog's health (much less any human's health). Although dogs are supposed to exercise and walk every day, a dog's stride is shorter than a human's, so it has to take more steps than a human to keep pace. The trail was also set up for human strides, and on sections of trail over boulders and climbing on rocks, there were spots where humans could go but dogs couldn't. Do you want to constantly worry about making sure your pet can climb over boulders or not get hurt somewhere along the trail?

The pets that hikers bring along weren't the only animals in the forest. There were plenty of wild animals who would either look at a dog as a tasty snack or run away for fear of being attacked. Most hikers wanted to see wildlife when they hiked, but bringing a dog greatly reduced their chances of seeing anything. To add to that, some people are also allergic to dogs, so by you bringing your dog on the journey, you are encroaching on their space and possibly putting them in harm's way. One more detriment was that we (humans) can bury our poop and we understand that there are places where and where not to go to the bathroom. Dogs don't understand the difference, and they go wherever they want to. To add to that, most owners don't clean up their dog's poop, and there were several times along the trail where I stepped on a fresh pile of dog droppings because it wasn't cleaned up. All in all, I think it is better off to leave your furry companions at home while undergoing a magical experience like hiking the Appalachian Trail.

Thru Hiking as a Weight-Loss Program

You might be surprised to know that there were very few hikers on the trail who were extremely thin-cut string beans like you might expect. There were people of all kinds of ages and body types on the trail, and although some people looked like they had no business being out on the trail, some hiked surprisingly fast. But there were also those like Ronnie from Israel, who fell on the much slower side of the spectrum.

Regardless of your height or weight, hiking the trail requires a massive number of calories. While a typical American is supposed to eat 2,000 to 2,500 calories per day, hikers typically eat between 4,000 and 6,000 calories, while bigger and faster hikers approach 8,000 or 9,000 calories per day. All those calories means that a hiker has to eat more every day, which means they have to carry more pack weight in food. I typically ate two to four pounds of food daily, which meant that my pack was extra heavy right after I resupplied. Some hikers didn't want to carry all this extra food with them on the trail, so they chose to consume less food during hiking days. Instead, every few days when they got into town, they gorged on food to try to make up for the caloric shortfall they experienced while hiking. While carrying more food slowed me down, it saved money because I bought all my food from grocery stores instead of restaurants and my body wasn't constantly caught between being overfull and starved for calories.

Despite how many calories I consumed on my hike, I was still bound to lose weight. I was in shape from basketball season, so I didn't anticipate losing much more than perhaps ten pounds in total. Before hitting the trail, I weighed in at about 230 pounds, but by the time I reached Massachusetts, I found that I was down to 225 pounds. I was blown away by my weight after I summited Katahdin, when I found that I was down to around 205 pounds. When my parents first saw me, they instantly noticed how gaunt my face looked, and they said I looked slightly better than a walking skeleton.

When I thought about the reason I didn't lose much weight in the first section but I lost much more later, I came up with a legitimate explanation. I attributed my initial weight loss to burning most of the limited body fat I had and simultaneous strengthening my leg muscles. This explains how I would have lost perhaps fifteen pounds (fat burn), but I gained ten pounds back (muscle development). By the end of the second portion of the trip, I noticed that my upper-body strength was gone. I assumed that my weight loss for the second portion was due to burning my arm and shoulder muscles for energy rather than carrying them around as extra weight. Perhaps it was also because the resupply stops were further spaced apart or I ran out of food on the last day of the Hundred Mile Wilderness, but these would only have slightly contributed to my unintended weight loss.

On the Pacific Crest Trail, I was particularly worried about losing weight like I did at the end of the Appalachian Trail, so I made sure to pack extra food. I ate plenty while I was hiking the PCT, and I never had a shortage or was in danger of running out of food (like I did several times on the AT). In the three weeks I spent in the Cascades, I came home and found that instead of losing weight, I put on two pounds compared to my pre-trail weight. That weight gain was probably because I hadn't developed hiker hunger yet, so my body wasn't as calorically starved as it would have been a month later.

Trail Legs

Speaking of development, one of the most interesting adaptions my body went through on the Appalachian Trail was the growth of my "trail legs." While it wasn't an overnight change, there was a span of a week that I went from cruising at a maximum speed of 2.5 miles per hour to the next week at 3.5 miles per hour. That was a huge difference for me, and it allowed me to hike faster and for longer periods. When I spent my first couple of days trying to keep up with The Northern Horde, I wondered if I would ever be able to keep pace with them. They told me to keep waiting until my trail legs developed, and when they did, I would be able to hike as fast as them.

Most hikers develop their legs after two weeks of hiking, but mine took a little longer than that. In New Jersey, I saw the first signs of my trail legs developing, and a few days later in New York, I was a completely different hiker. It was nothing short of a miracle, and I noticed the change in the middle of the day. I was hiking uphill over rough terrain when I suddenly realized that I should've already stopped and caught my breath. However, I wasn't tired and didn't worry about stopping. It was a beautiful feeling to know I could hike at whatever pace I wanted to, and I enjoyed that feeling for several weeks after I finished the trail.

Fording Streams and Rivers

Before I started the trail, I was worried about having to ford a river. I had no idea there were any fords on the Appalachian Trail until I opened my trail guidebook and saw the word "ford." I didn't even know what the word 'ford' meant until I looked it up. I saw it written next to about a dozen streams or rivers in Maine, and I feared the worst. The feeling of fear almost kept me from the ever hiking the trail, and I thought about quitting then and there. I knew I didn't swim well, and with a 50 pound pack on my back, my odds of making it across a large stream were low. Inadvertently, I also freaked out beforehand by watching several videos of hikers crossing swollen streams in the Sierra Nevada snowmelt in California. I watched the hikers get swept away in the current, and I wondered if the streams ever got that bad on the Appalachian Trail.

A few miles before I reached the first ford, I still worried. I didn't know how to ford a river, so I asked several of the SOBO hikers, "How do you ford a river?" Their response was, "You'll figure it out pretty quickly." Wow, what a total waste of my time! When I reached the first ford, the West Branch Piscataquis River, I heard a thunderstorm a few minutes away. I quickly sat on the riverbank, stowed away my socks and soles in my pack, and put my shoes back on. I also packed my wallet and cell phone inside a watertight bag in the brain of my pack in case I fell into the river. The anticipation was killing me as I slowly touched my shoe into the cool river water.

As I heard thunder getting closer, I started wading out into the river. The first half of the stream was shallow and easy to get across, but midway through, the streambed dropped off and the current picked up. I started to panic as I edged my way across the river. The cold water bit into my legs, and my feet were numb after standing in the water for a minute, but I slowly inched across the worst stretch of rapids. I had to kick several stones out of my way so they didn't shift under my weight, but I finally reached the other side of the river after a long and painful two minutes. My legs and shoes were dripping, and when I took my shoes off and turned them upside-down, a stream of water poured out from inside. Wet and exhausted, I continued walking down the trail in the thunderstorm with my squishy shoes until I reached the next stream.

This is how just about every crossing went. After hiking across the calf or knee-deep river, I waited on the far side and dried off before continuing on. When I crossed Little Wilson Stream and Big Wilson Stream in the Hundred Mile Wilderness, I was especially worried because it had rained for a week straight. The streams were over their banks, and I waded through waist-deep water (and remember that I am 6'9" too!) to reach the other side. Those two first crossings in the Hundred Mile Wilderness were the worst, but the others were still scary at times. The only pleasant ford I had was the (ironically named) West Branch Pleasant River. Although I worried for days about fording rivers, they didn't turn out to be as bad as I thought, although they were a big danger. Looking back on it, if a crossing would have been too difficult to do, the Appalachian Trail Conservancy would do something about it, like how they ferry hikers across the Kennebec River. Additionally, if 70-year-old hikers were able to ford these rivers, I see no reason why I couldn't do the same!

Hiking the Pacific Crest Trail

When I made my preparations for my journey on the PCT, I made a schedule of my trek, which was supposed to start on June 5th and finish around August 18th. Because of the weather and other factors, I wasn't able to be out on trail at the beginning or last until August. And although I planned to hike 1500 miles, I only ended up walking about 300 of those miles.

My plan was to start at the Oregon-Washington border in Cascade Locks and hike SOBO until I finished the section in southern California at Kennedy Meadows. Despite all the preparation I did and the prior experience I had (from hiking the Appalachian Trail), I still wasn't able to deal with the conditions I faced on the Pacific Crest Trail. The biggest contributor to my demise by far was the weather that occurred months prior to me hitting the trail.

2019 Winter Weather

The Sierra Nevada and Cascade Range winter of 2019 was the second snowiest year in the last two decades, only surpassed by the snow totals from 2017. December and January were both warmer than usual and the snow totals didn't accumulate as much, but the following months were brutal. In February and March, the West Coast was hit by round-after-round of storms in a phenomenon known as a "Pineapple Express". These storms dumped feet of snow at the higher elevations the trail was at, and cities along the coast that rarely see snow (such as Seattle and Portland) each saw over a foot of snowfall due to a combination of the extreme cold and plentiful moisture. The months of April and May weren't much better, and although the temperatures were slightly warmer, they were still mostly below freezing, which didn't help melt the myriad of snow along the trail. There were parts of the trail in Oregon that were still increasing their snow depth into late May, and snow fell on portions of the trail well into June and July.

When I looked at the long-range winter forecast in October, the forecasters were predicting a strong El Niño during the winter. A situation like that meant that the Pacific Northwest would remain warmer and drier than usual, which was exactly the forecast that I was looking for. Unfortunately, that weather pattern only lasted until January. February was a rough month for me, as I helplessly waited in my room and saw the incredulous snow totals for storm after storm. I hoped for a light or average snow year, but I came to the realization that that was less likely to happen by the day. I remember looking at a forecast for Drakesbad Ranch in Lassen Volcanic National Park, which showed a predicted nine feet of snow to fall in a 48-hour period on February 25-26th! Incredible snow totals like that were commonplace throughout the winter, and the snow resorts on were actually seeing too much snow fall. In February, Mammoth Mountain picked up a record 24 feet of snow, and the unrelenting snowfall allowed the resort to remain open well into August. Timberline Lodge (on the slopes of Mount Hood) had snow at 6000 feet well into July, well past when I hiked past.

As I mentioned earlier, 2017 was the year that the most snow fell in the Sierra Nevadas, but it wasn't able to break the drought that California was in. However, the snow during the winter of 2019 fell statewide, and although more than ¾ of the state was in moderate drought in November, the entire state was drought-free by April. This broke the longest-lasting drought in California history, which had persisted since 2011. Although it was extremely unfortunate for me and the 1000 (or so) other hikers attempting the Pacific Crest Trail, having access to fresh water for millions is more important than my opportunity to hike the PCT.

Gearing up for the Trip

I knew there were fewer resupply spots along the PCT and they were going to be more expensive than food on the AT, so I decided to mail food to various points along the trail. Because of these maildrops, I was able to pick food that I enjoyed, and I didn't have to worry about whatever selection I found in nearby stores. I saved money on the cost per unit food, as food in the small camp stores was ridiculously expensive or nonexistent at some spots. I also saved time by not worrying about spending a day off the trail to purchase supplies. That was especially helpful at times when I was 20-30 miles from the nearest town. Traveling to the town and back would have added a lot of time and stress to my hike.

I also decided to swap out some gear before the trip. My goal was to reduce my pack weight a more manageable number. Instead of the 32 pound baseweight I carried on the Appalachian Trail, I planned for a more reasonable 25 pound baseweight on the Pacific Crest Trail. My strategy was to increase my overall speed because I had to traverse longer distances between stops, and I was able to do this because my lower pack weight allowed me to travel faster and longer.

Hitting the Trail

After I mailed my food to several locations on the trail, I flew from Pittsburgh to Portland on June 8th. My flight arrived at 2 AM and I spent the night with a friend of a distant relative. In the morning, I took an hour-long bus ride to Cascade Locks. As we drove through the Columbia River Gorge, my jaw dropped at the scenery, which served as a wake-up call for the natural beauty I was to see on the trail. After taking my initial pictures with the Bridge of the Gods, I ventured across it. I was only on the trail for a few minutes, when I already crossed into another state, Washington!

I have a fear of heights, so walking across that bridge was difficult for me. Although most bridges have concrete or asphalt paving, this bridge only had metal grates, which were the only thing separating me from a long fall to the river below. To add to my confusion, the bridge had no pedestrian sidewalk, so I was forced to walk in the active traffic lanes, and I held on for dear life when the bridge shook from a car passing. Regardless of my fear, I enjoyed seeing the bridge, and now I know why it was a highlight they showed in the movie *Wild*.

Once I crossed the bridge back into Oregon, it was time for me to begin hiking southbound. About a half mile later, the trail split off with the Eagle Creek Alternate Trail. I wanted to hike the alternate trail, an area known for picturesque waterfalls and steep ravines, but there was a fire in 2017 that decimated the area. The Eagle Creek Fire started when a teenager illegally lit fireworks off in the forest, and the fire that ensued burned 50,000 acres. The alternate trail was still closed even a year and a half after the fire started, so I had no choice but to continue hiking on the PCT. It wasn't until the following day that I saw the full extent of the fire.

Hiking the PCT in Oregon

One thing that I immediately noticed was that the forest contained some of the largest trees I had ever seen. I have seen the tallest and largest trees in the eastern United States, but these trees dwarfed over their eastern counterparts (and these were only Douglas fir trees). It was a long climb out of the Columbia River Gorge (the lowest point on the PCT), but once the trail reached clearings at the top, I was amazed by the expansive views. By the second day, I had already seen better views from the trail than I had for the entire AT. I looked to the north and saw Mount Adams, St. Helens, and Rainier, and to my south at Mount Hood. As the trail approached the latter mountain, it appeared ever more ominous and snow-covered. I heard from other hikers that the snowpack on the mountainside was bad, so I made the decision to cross it early in the morning when the snow was cooler and easier to trek across.

Before I reached the mountain base, though, I had more terrain and streams I needed to cross. I bear-hugged a giant log as I inched over Mud Fork, then I passed through what appeared to be a basalt desert until I reached Ramona Falls. The waterfall was beautiful, and the mist blowing off the basalt columns felt incredible after a hot day of hiking. The final crossing I had was Sandy River, and luckily someone else made a makeshift log bridge. The water that fed into the river was all from melting snow and glaciers, so the river would have been very cold and dangerous to ford, at an ice-cold 35°F. I camped by the side of a nearby creek (Rushing Water Creek) and went out just before sunset to take pictures of the sun reflecting on Mount Hood.

Once I started climbed the mountain in the morning, there were continuous fields of snow starting at about 5000 feet. Although a majority of the snow had melted, the continuous freeze-thaw cycles made the surface extremely slippery. The slopes were very treacherous and there were plenty of places where the snow had blown over a section of trail and frozen into a block making my journey difficult. Crossing the icy patches would have been easier if I had crampons or micro spikes, but the manufacturers told me they don't make anything for size 18. Because of that, I was forced to trudge through the snow in a pair of waterproofed trail runners.

Further up the mountain, I crossed Lost Creek, and found myself…lost. The trail disappeared completely in the snow, and there were no tracks I could follow. I tried to use my phone's GPS to determine my location relative to the trail, but the steep slopes in the canyon caused the GPS to be unable to pinpoint my location. After being lost and panicking for 30 minutes, I finally located the trail and continued on to my next obstacle. When I tried to rock hop across Zigzag River, I slipped and fell into the river, so I spent the next hour hiking while dripping and freezing in the glacial water. After I ate lunch and stared at the summit, I met a few guests who were staying at Timberline Lodge, so I knew I must be getting close. The remaining two miles weren't on difficult terrain, but it was difficult following the trail as it meandered through snowfields. To make matters worse, it was also warm and sunny out, which caused the snow to melt and become slushy, and the glare of the sun off the snow blinded me as I labored towards Timberline Lodge.

I reached the lodge by early afternoon and picked up my first resupply package there. I spent twenty minutes sitting on a rock stuffing the food into my pack, and it felt strange to suddenly see people walking around. I saw perhaps a dozen people in the last five days, and suddenly I was surrounded by throngs of people. While I was there, I saw a family that drove up to from Los Angeles to the lodge with their kids. They had never seen snow before, and I watched them fire snowballs at each other and build their first snowman. Once I got sick and tired of seeing all the people around me, I said goodbye to Jeff (who I had been hiking on-and-off with) and headed down the mountain. Off in the distance, I saw Mount Jefferson and the Three Sisters looming with their vast snowfields.

Once I descended Mount Hood and passed the historic Barlow Toll Road, the trail flattened out. The scenery that I was used to started to disappear, and it felt like I was hiking through another green tunnel. The trail wound through small hills and valleys, and I saw Little Crater Lake and Timothy Lake. Because the trail had such sparse tree cover and last few days were warm and sunny, I found I was getting sunburnt while walking on the trail. The blinding sun didn't stop even through the trail crossed into Warm Springs Indian Reservation, and for a 23 mile stretch, the trail corridor was a mere 200 feet wide. The forest composition changed too. The northern side of Mount Hood had large, full-grown trees, which gave the area a cool, moist microclimate. However, the southern side was dry, rocky, and sparsely populated with scraggly pine trees. Water was scarce along the trail, and when I found it, it was always infested with mosquitoes. The trail emerged from the Native American reservation at Olallie Lake Resort, a quaint camp situated at the foot of Olallie Butte and on the edge of a lake. I pitched my tent for the night and ate dinner as I watched the sun set against Mount Jefferson.

A day before, I had camped at Warm Springs River and met a northbound thru hiker named Cosmo. She had just got back on the trail near Olallie Lake Resort after finishing a section in Northern California. She reported that the section to the south of Olallie Lake was impassable and that no one had hiked through the section yet. I frowned when I heard that news, as it meant I had two choices: to risk hiking a dangerous section nobody has hiked yet or to skip ahead and hike a different section of the trail. I looked at a map that night and saw there was a small forest road that I could take to bail off the trail just past Olallie Lake. As I approached the bail point, there were portions of the PCT where the trail disappeared and became a small lake. I waded through the water to reach the other side, only to find another pond in front of me. As the trail reached 5500 feet elevation, the snowfields started, and I found myself trudging through feet of snow. I also got word from another PCT hiker that someone had attempted that trail section and fallen off the trail, which was the final straw for me. I decided that it wasn't worth getting me injured or killed out in the woods, so I called my parents. I told them I was still alive and that I would contact them when I reached the nearest town, Detroit, in two days. I broke off from the trail at the bail point, and I walked a portion of the 26 miles into town when I got a hitch from Geoff and Sylvie.

Hiking the PCT in California

As things stood, I was in quite a pickle. Thankfully, I met Geoff that day and he picked me up, because I don't know how different things would have turned out had that not happened. I spent two days with him in Salem, OR, and then I took a Greyhound all the way to Redding, CA. From there, I rode in an Uber to a snow-free section of the trail, which started in Old Station, CA. My new revised plan was to hike from Old Station to Dunsmuir, and the goal was by the time I reached there, more of the snow would have melted in southern Oregon and I would continue hiking towards Crater Lake. It wasn't possible for me to hike anywhere southward, as most of the trail in California was impassible until late July or August, and the parts that I could do were near the Mexican border through the scorching desert (which didn't sound like fun in the summer).

But before I could think about hiking in the snow in Oregon, I had to deal with a very different landscape. Instead of vast snowfields, I found myself hiking through the desert. On my first day back on the trail, I trekked across Hat Creek Rim, a dry section known for extremely limited water sources. To make matters worse, a series of fires had decimated the landscape several years ago, so there was no forest cover left to shade the beating sun. Both factors combined for a brutally hot day, as the temperature was in the 90's while I trudged through the desert. When I finally found a tree, I waited under it for the hottest part of the day to pass. I spent the remainder of the day stumbling over much of the trail until I reached a water source at the end of a 22 mile stretch without water.

That night I accidentally set my tent up on a beehive, and I got stung multiple times by yellowjackets. After getting off Hat Creek Rim, the water sources were closer, and about every ten miles I found a spring or stream. At the same time, I read snow depth reports that showed the snowpack was resilient and melting at a much slower rate than I anticipated, which was a disappointment. It took a few days, but over time, I slowly realized that I was probably going to have to stop my hike when I reached Dunsmuir, because no more of the trail was snow-free.

That was still several days away, so I focused on what was directly in front of me. After I saw how beautiful Burney Falls was, my mood improved, and I started hiking faster again. I took a break later that that day along the side of the trail and I sat down on a rock. Like usual, I grabbed a granola bar and some trail mix and started eating it when I felt something run across my arm. I looked down and saw my arms were coated in red ants. Fearful, I looked down my shirt, and saw them crawling all over me. I hurriedly jumped up and stripped off my clothes in the middle of the trail. Although the ant bites didn't hurt, they were a nuisance as I plucked them off one by one. They were also persistent and held onto my shirt tightly. After spending a solid fifteen minutes cleaning them off my clothes, I put my clothes back on and continued hiking. I was glad no one else passed me, because they would have been scarred for life after seeing me standing in the middle of the trail in my birthday suit.

The weather pattern in the mountains was also hot and dry, and CalFire declared a Red Flag Warning for high fire danger. I was extremely cautious when I used my stove, but I wasn't prepared for what I saw ahead. Instead of staring ahead at a wildfire, I instead saw a snowy ridge in front of me. Two hikers alerted me a few miles back that there was snow ahead, but I just laughed at them because I was told by numerous hikers (including Cosmo) that I was on a snow-free section of trail. So when I reached Mushroom Rock and saw all of the snow, I knew I was in for another tough section.

The Tipping Point

The snow covered about two miles of the trail. The first half mile was along the mountainside with a myriad of snow chutes (areas of snow on a steep-sloped cliff with a long fall) and the second part was mostly a ridge walk for one and a half miles along the northern edge of the mountain. Slowly but surely, I crossed the first section, despite the snow slope ranging between 30 and 55°. I took a break after I finished the first section of snow, and I figured that the remainder would go by quickly. I was wrong....

Not a minute after I started hiking again, I saw another steep chute and I had no choice but to walk across it. There were postholes through the snow, so I knew people had already hiked across this section. I gingerly walked onto the snow and halfway through it, I stepped on a posthole, when suddenly my footing gave way in the wet snow and I started to slide down the slope! I started gaining speed and frantically looked at the boulders at the bottom of the slope. I knew I had seconds to grab something before I crashed into the rocks. I spotted the top of a fir tree sticking out of the snow, and I grabbed ahold of it with all my strength. The tree slowed me down, and I stood there dangling from the branch. Next, I used my feet to kick out footings for my shoes from the icy snow. Then, I slowly inched my way off the chute and back to the same side I started on. I climbed up the 20 feet I just fell and repositioned myself to traverse the same icy chute again.

I looked again for another way around this snowy area, but there were no other options. I somehow found the strength to continue and I cautiously made my way past the spot I had wiped out on. I took another deep breath and slid off the snowy patch onto solid ground. The remaining ridge walk was much easier, and once I passed the two miles, I was out of the snow. However, the experience scarred me, and I called my parents right away and told them how I just slipped off a cliff. I told them that I was done dealing with the snow and I knew it wasn't worth continuing on because there was such a high probability of myself getting hurt. After all, the PCT will still be there next year! I let them know I was mentally finished hiking and that I was going to come home when I reached Dunsmuir. With a heavy heart knowing my hike would end in a few days, I continued on for the remaining forty miles.

The last two nights I spent on the trail were particularly restless, as I slept alone at campsites that were loaded with signs of bear activity. I didn't have any visitors either night, but on my second to last day, I had a run-in with a rattlesnake along the side of the trail. That just cemented my belief that I was mentally finished with the trail, and I bought my plane tickets home that night. And to make matters worse, I got poison oak while hiking near the McCloud River. I stumbled out of the forest near Dunsmuir as a wreck, but knew my excursion wasn't quite over yet.

Journeying from Dunsmuir to Pittsburgh

When I got to Dunsmuir, I decided to stay at Crossroads, a hostel run by Kelly McCree. There, I met Tropicana and Farmer's Market, two siblings who were thru hiking the trail together. So far, they had completed pieces of the trail and were planning to stitch the other pieces of trail together when the snow conditions improved later. I was disappointed to tell them I was leaving, but I already bought my plane tickets to fly back to Pittsburgh. But before I purchased them, I checked to see the cost for me to rent a car for a week to drive and see some of the sights I missed on the trail. But, the cost of myself renting a car for the week was an outlandish $1,100. At that price, I could have driven from Pittsburgh all the way out there and back!

I scheduled a day between when I finished the trail and when I needed to be in Medford to fly home. Naturally, I decided to try another hike that day, so I planned to hike Black Butte. I first saw the sharp-pointed mountain on my Greyhound ride from Salem, OR to Redding, CA and at the time, I wondered what the view was like from the top. To get to Black Butte, I had to walk further into town, and when I stood by the on-ramp for Interstate 5, I got a hitch from two locals nicknamed Canada and Robin. Not only were they nice enough to take me to Mount Shasta, they also took me all the way to the trailhead, which was many miles out of their way and down several dirt roads. When I arrived, I saw about twenty cars in the parking lot, so I figured I would have no problem getting a ride back to the highway. I was wrong again and as I was ascending the mountain, I saw a group of about thirty people coming down from the summit.

After enjoying the panoramic view from the summit, I made my way back down and passed several people headed back to their car. After I started walking back on the dirt roads, a couple picked me up and gave me a ride back to the paved Everitt Memorial Highway. From there, I got another hitch from a lady who took me to see Mount Shasta Big Springs. That spring was the headwaters of the Sacramento River, and when I was there, people from all the surrounding towns brought buckets and canteens to fill up with the fresh spring water. She dropped me off in nearby Weed, CA, and I waited along the side of the on-ramp for Interstate 5 to hitch a ride. I kid you not, the second car that passed me stopped and asked me if I needed a ride. She was driving up to Seattle and she moved all her stuff around so I could fit in the front seat. After talking to her for the hour and a half car ride, I found out that she was headed to Washington to start hiking southbound on the PCT. She told me she thought I was a PCT hiker, but she was very confused why I was in Weed, some twenty miles from the nearest trail town. She had just sold her belongings in San Francisco and was planning to leave her car with a friend in Seattle while she began hiking at Rainy Pass. Getting the hitch from her for that entire distance was such a huge help, as I was able to take just one hitch all the way from Weed to Medford instead of spending hours getting several hitches.

I arrived hours before I planned to get there, and I used that time to take plenty of showers to try and get some of the trail stink off me. I was also breaking out in poison oak, so it was nice being able to shower with soap and water to properly treat the bumps that had spread across my body. And just like that, bright and early the next morning, I was back on a plane bound for PIT. My first flight was from Medford to Seattle, then the next one was to Salt Lake City, and finally on to Pittsburgh. The plane landed in the middle of a thunderstorm, and I was shocked by the sight of the rain. After all, I hadn't any rain or snow fall from the sky in the weeks that I spent on the West Coast. When we finally disembarked, I met my parents, gave them a big hug, and breathed a giant sigh of relief.

Leaving My Trace

L eave No Trace (LNT) principles are of the utmost importance for long-distance hikers, as our impact on the environment is much greater than a day hiker's impact. Although hikers rarely talk about LNT principles, they are the "unwritten rules," guidelines that hikers try to follow. Now, I would be a complete hypocrite if I said I always followed LNT principles, but I tried to follow them as best as I could. In this chapter, I explore each of the principles, ways to follow them, and times when I wasn't up to the challenge.

Planning Ahead and Preparing

This kind of goes without saying. As with anything in life, you should always plan ahead and prepare because you never can be sure what is going to happen. As Murphy's Law states, 'Anything that can go wrong will go wrong.' Preparation is an easy way to make sure that a hike of any duration is a fun, exploratory journey. It is important to have all the necessary gear for the hike, regardless of the duration. I prefer carrying more gear than I probably will need as a precaution. Out in the woods, especially in the wilderness, you never know how things are going to end up, and it is bets to be prepared for the worst. Even if you had the opportunity to be rescued, rescuers might be hours or days away, and your safety is in your hands. Although you might not need the additional gear, that possibility of saving your life outweighs the extra weight that that gear requires.

When I hiked the Appalachian and Pacific Crest Trails, I left a schedule of my hike with my parents. Although the schedule I made didn't exactly line up with the distances I covered each day, they provided my parents with a good estimation of when I planned to reach the next trail town. I also looked at topographical maps on the trail, so I gave them estimations about when I would have cell coverage next and when I would reach the next road, town, etc. By preparing ahead of time, I am certain that I helped keep my parents from panicking and I also provided them with an estimation of where I was in case things went badly (like if I fell off a cliff...).

Knowing trail conditions was also crucial to my hike, and I routinely checked various websites and talked with hikers to keep myself up to date on the latest conditions. One thing I worried about when I hiked the PCT was the possibility of getting caught in a stretch of wilderness when a wildfire approached. I heard plenty of stories about hikers being stranded or having to be rescued from wildfires, so I knew that wasn't a position I wanted to be in. By knowing my surroundings, I was able to keep myself safe and even avert disaster. Before leaving for the trip, I researched types of tree leaves that could be safely eaten, but I never imagined that would come in handy. However, I found myself in the Hundred Mile Wilderness running out of food, so I was forced to eat leaves to sustain myself for half of a day.

Food wasn't the only resource that was critical to my hike. Water was abundant through many stretches of the trail, but there were places where water sources were spaced ten to fifteen miles apart. On Hat Creek Rim, I was forced to hike 22 miles without water through the scorching desert heat. Without my trail guide, I would have had no idea how crucial it was to stock up on water before the dry stretch. Despite the greater availability of water along the Appalachian Trail, there were several stretches where I ran out of water. I arrived at several springs only to discover they had dried up. In situations like that, although it would have been annoying to fill up with water at more streams and thus carry more weight, it would have been worthwhile when I found myself out of water and thirty. It was (and is) important to never carry just enough water to reach the next source, which is exactly why planning ahead and preparing were necessary.

Traveling and Camping on Durable Surfaces

Over the course of a thru hike, a hiker takes more than 4 million steps. When I hiked half of the trail, I wore a Fitbit Charge and over my 68 days on the trail, it registered that I took 2,675,771 steps. Now that was quite a lot of steps! In those two months, I hiked almost two times more than the average American walks in a year! Because of all those steps, it was important that I walked on a durable surface. In just about every place, the trail stands out because it was well-marked and worn in. With the thousands of people that hike the trail each year and the number of steps each hiker takes, the math shows why it is important to stay on the maintained trail. Going off-trail could have serious consequences, especially above tree line and in sensitive areas. In places like this, the vegetation is extremely fragile and can easily die from being trampled. Following posted instructions and scree walls in alpine environments are important to ensure that our children and grandchildren can see the same grandiose mountains we can.

I haven't always hiked on durable surfaces. In Vermud (where mud puddles were everywhere), I always tried to step around the puddles to keep my feet dry. Although my steps around a puddle make a miniscule impact, the hundreds or thousands of hikers that step around the same puddle make a huge difference, which leads to the surrounding vegetation being trampled. If a section of the trail gets too bad, the maintainers usually reroute the trail to another area or they submerge branches or rocks into the mud to allow hikers to walk through on a durable surface.

Camping on a durable surface is perhaps even more important than hiking on one. While hiking through the forest disturbs small sections at a time and is rarely noticeable after one incident, camping disturbs a large area and can be noticed after just one night. Because a hiker's tent (or hammock) is set in a fixed position, they take many more steps around the area where it was set up. The location for a camp site or stealth site should be well-used, with compact soil, and free from any live plants or branches. There are plenty of stealth campsites along the trail, and it was much better (and easier) for me to sleep at an existing campsite than to make one for myself.

When I was in a rush and just wanted to sleep for the night, I didn't always camp at an existing campsite. When I was hiking in the Whites, it was already dark out and I couldn't find an open tent site near Galehead Hut. All the other tent sites were taken, but eventually I found a patch of moss that was flat enough to set up my tent. After a rough night of sleep, I emerged from my tent in the morning and saw it was unrecognizable. Hundreds of slugs had slowly slunk onto my tent, which covered it in slime. I guess that was karma for me not camping at an existing campsite.

Disposing of Waste Properly

Finally we reached my favorite subject, poop! Before hiking the Appalachian Trail, I had never done my business in the woods, and imagined it would be disgusting. But after going in the woods for months on end, I found that I preferred going in the woods rather than a privy. Even though all animals defecate in the woods, doing my business in the woods could potentially be much more damaging than going in a privy, so it was important for hikers to follow some guidelines. If all went well, your poop would turn into usable soil, by being naturally decomposed by microbes in the forest floor. This is fairly similar to what happens in a privy along the trail. All the human poop is collected in a large container and combined with leaves and forest waste to start the decomposition. After several months of the microbes working, the waste matter would be spread along the forest floor as usable topsoil.

If you go on the forest floor, most sources recommend burying poop in a cat hole six inches deep and four inches wide. When I hiked the AT and PCT and had to go, I dug the hole, did my business, dropped my toilet paper in, then backfilled it with excess material from the forest floor. Here it is important to note that there are different rules at various parks, and some require you to pack out used toilet paper, and some even your poop! Although that seems like it takes LNT principles too far, I understand there are certain cases where that is warranted.

There are restrictions on where you should and should not dispose of your waste. Going to the bathroom near bodies of water is a big no-no for hikers, and people should urinate at least 50 feet from any water and poop 200 feet from any water source. Problems arise whenever hikers got to the bathroom near a body of water because the bacteria we excrete runoff into nearby water, where they multiply. A week later, when a thirsty hiker drinks from that bacteria-laden source, they might get *Giardia* or another waterborne illness. I always made sure to do my business away from water, as I wanted to leave the water sources cleaner than I found them. I was blessed to have good, clean drinking water during my journey, so took it upon myself to make sure that hikers after me could also enjoy the same crisp water that I had.

I didn't always follow the other rules about properly disposing my waste on the forest floor. While some hikers have an innate ability to know exactly when they needed to drop a deuce, I was not one of them. Some people knew that every day at 5:00 they were going to have to use the bathroom, so they were prepared for when the time came. Unfortunately, I wasn't one of those people with a "regular" cycle, and when I felt the urge to go, I knew I was in a race against time. I had about sixty seconds to stop hiking, grab everything I needed, and dig a hole. To make matters worse, I didn't carry a trowel with me, so I relied on loose rocks or sticks to dig my hole. While it saved a few ounces off my baseweight (and saved me from carrying around a shitty trowel), I couldn't always dig myself a hole. There were times when I couldn't dig deep enough into the topsoil or I there were no loose rocks or sticks to dig with. In those cases, I found myself pooping on the bare ground or a small depression. Afterwards, I formed a small mound with forest litter, so I made the most with the items I had at my disposal.

That was what I did when I needed to go while I was out hiking. Things at a shelter were generally better, and most times, I was able to make it to the privy or I found a spot in the woods when the time came. Pooping in the woods at a shelter wasn't always the best idea, though, because there were always other hikers around. I always worried about someone seeing me doing my business along the side of the trail. One big difference between going along the AT and the PCT was the amount of brush in the forest understory. On the AT, there were plenty of bushes and small trees that provided some privacy, but they were nonexistent on the PCT. No one has rounded a corner on either trail and walked across me doing my business, so I can't complain.

"Pack it in, pack it out." Considering all the times I have been out hiking, that phrase is one that always sticks in my head. Although, I saw that sign at virtually every trailhead along the AT, I found a surprisingly large amount of waste stacked up at the trailhead. There the waste was, waiting for a garbage truck that would never come. Long-distance hikers are cognizant of the role that we play in keeping the trail litter-free. A vast majority of us end up picking up and disposing of much more trash than we leave behind. There were times I felt my heart break when I spotted water bottles or wrappers along the side of the trail. I usually bent over, picked up their garbage, and packed it out with the rest of trash I generated. I was in a much better mood hiking along a litter-free trail than when I saw trash scattered about.

Leaving What I Found

The fourth LNT principle reminds me of when I was a child and played on a giant rock pile. I wanted to take and keep all the cool and interesting rocks, but my parents convinced me to leave them behind. They said to keep them there so other kids could enjoy them too. There were so many spots along the AT and PCT that I thought, "Wouldn't it be nice to have a souvenir to remind me of this moment?" Although it may have been nice to have a rock to remind me of a place, if everyone who visited that place took a rock, there would be nothing left in a few years.

I always followed this rule except when I reached the tallest peak in each state. I am also a highpointer, so I try to hike to the tallest point of each states in the United States. To commemorate each state that I summit, I take a rock as a souvenir and write on it the mountain name, height, and date ascended. When I was hiking up to the peak of, say, Mount Greylock (the tallest peak in Massachusetts), I looked for a rock that reminded me of the mountain. After I finished hiking the trail, I added that rock to my collection. I tried to minimize my damage by taking only one rock, and I was also encouraged to take a small rock because I had to carry it with me all the way to Katahdin. Along the same lines, I collect rocks and minerals, so when I visited some of the various mines I went to along the trail, I tried to save some samples for myself. Although I didn't follow this LNT principle, I tried to limit the disturbance I made.

Minimizing Campfire Impacts

"Only you can prevent forest fires!" While Smokey the Bear may sound cheesy saying the lines, it holds true. Most fires are caused by humans, and too many wildfires are started after a campfire escapes from a firepit or when someone plays around with fire. The fire danger was lesser on the Appalachian Trail, but it was a huge concern on the Pacific Crest Trail. As I spent days walking through burn scars along the trail, I got a sense of how damaging one person's misdeeds can turn out to be.

The possibility of starting a forest fire shouldn't be the only reason to limit the number of times you have a fire. Fire remnants are eyesores, and when a hiker passes through a campsite and notices half-burnt logs, they wonder why someone else messed up the campsite. To prevent excess pieces of wood remaining after a fire, only burn pieces of wood smaller in diameter than your wrist. Speaking from my experience, when I burnt larger pieces of wood, I rarely was able to burn them completely. And those times they finally did, it was hours after I started the campfire. The remaining partially burnt logs persisted in the morning, long after I finished having the campfire. I burnt smaller material (such as sticks and twigs) to ashes, but sometimes I couldn't burn some of the larger pieces of wood before I wanted to go to bed. In those circumstances, I drowned the fire with water before I left it unattended or hit the hay. By ensuring the fire was completely out, I helped prevent a potential forest fire.

Although there were some days when I was in the mood and had time to make a fire, not all days were suitable for fires. I avoided having fires during dry spells or when vegetation appeared to be drying out, as these were signs that an escaped ember could light something else ablaze. The wind was also a nuisance when making a fire because it blew ashes and smoke around and into my face, so I wanted a wind-free night to have a fire on. On the other side of the spectrum, nothing burned if it rained for the past couple of days, so at times like that, it was best to save my energy and go to bed instead of fighting to maintain the fire. Days suited for a fire are "Goldilocks" days, meaning they are spaced between the forest being too wet and too dry, along with limited wind. Sitting around the campfire with friends can be a magical experience, but it also should be done responsibly.

Respecting Wildlife

The thing I want to point out here is that wildlife is…wild. Animals found out in the forest are not domesticated. They have been trained for generations and generations to survive and fend for themselves. Trust me, they don't need people to feed them. Feeding animals causes them to become reliant on humans. Usually, an animal that has been fed becomes a nuisance that needs to be killed to protect visitors. I arrived at a shelter late one afternoon and saw a group of deer grazing near a shelter. They remained in the vicinity of the shelter throughout the night and were still there in the morning. While it may seem cool to have a video of a deer eating food out of your hands, the deer ends up with the worst of it. Like I said, the deer will probably end up being killed and you could face hefty fines for feeding wildlife.

Keeping your distance from animals is also a priority. Just as you wouldn't want a bear standing next to you, I am sure a bear wouldn't want you next to it. Instead of taking photos from 10 feet away, perhaps stand 25 feet away and zoom in on your camera to take a picture of the animal. That's what the zoom feature is used for, right? Wild animal behavior is too erratic to trust, so I never break this LNT principle. I know I am better off keeping my distance from the animals and enjoying them in their natural setting.

Being Considerate of Others

"Treat others the way you want to be treated." The Golden Rule applies to hikers too, and although hikers see many less people than in our "normal lives," human interactions are perhaps more important on the trail. Most hikers I met were extremely peaceful and were hiking the trail for the same reason as me: to get away from it all, enjoy the sounds of nature, and make memories with the trees. However, there were a select few people who were caused trouble for more than one hiker. I was sitting on a bunk at Alec Kennedy Shelter in Pennsylvania after a long, rainy day when a fight broke out between two hikers. It started as an argument about who was going to sleep on which bunk, but it ended with the disgruntled hiker receiving a punch to the face and breaking his nose. Luckily, other hikers and I broke it up after the scuffle started and the grumpy, disgruntled hiker, Mikey, moved on with a bloody nose.

Thankfully that was the worst thing that I witnessed on the trail, and just about everyone else was much more courteous and respectful. Just about everyone else was accommodating and looked out for others. After all, all of us hikers faced the same challenges every day. We shared all that we had: food, gear, and (perhaps most importantly) advice with each other. However, there were times when people didn't realize they were rambling on incessantly about unimportant things. When I was in the Bigelows, an older hiker stopped me and just started talking to me. He tried to give me some advice and me told me that I was hiking the trail incorrectly and I needed to rethink my hiking strategy. I looked shocked when he told me that, but I kept my mouth shut, knowing it wasn't worth it to respond. I would hope that after hiking 1000 miles, I would have a pretty good idea how to backpack, but in his eyes, I was doing it all wrong.

Being considerate also involves following etiquette while hiking. I avoided talking on the phone or listening to music out loud. If I knew I was going to get a phone call or listen to music, I put in my set of headphones and did that quietly, to avoid distracting other hikers. The first time I listened to music with my music blasting, a hiker passed me and gave me a disappointing look. From then on, I switched to headphones. I also tried to avoid taking any phone calls or using my phone when I was around other hikers, to ensure they had a good wilderness experience. By executing these small changes to my hiking routine, I like to think that I helped brighten someone else's day and made their experience more enjoyable.

A State-by-State View of the Appalachian Trail

T he Appalachian Trail passes through fourteen different states, and the section I hiked included eight of those states. Each of the borders were clearly marked, but there wasn't always a glaring difference that I noticed at any of the crossings. Although there was very little difference between some states, it was a huge mental boost to know that I crossed into yet another state. This feeling helped propel me to Maine, and along the way, I hiked through states that I enjoyed more than others. After reading this section, ponder on which states you think I enjoyed the most and which ones I enjoyed the least.

Pennsylvania: Rocksylvania

"I feel like I haven't seen a single view in Pennsylvania because I've been so busy staring at the ground to avoid tripping over rocks."

- Craft E

When hikers take the post-hiking annual survey of the Appalachian Trail, almost everybody lists Pennsylvania as their least favorite state. With endless rock fields and extremely rough terrain, most hikers can't wait to get out of

Pennsylvania and into New Jersey. The fallacy they face is that there are still rocky sections in New Jersey and northward, despite the notion that the rocks end at the Delaware River. Although the rocks north of PA may not be pointed and dig into your feet, but they are still littered about the trail all the way to the summit of Katahdin.

Most hikers enter Pennsylvania at Pen Mar Park (the PA-MD border), but my journey began about twenty miles north in Caledonia State Park because of flooding in Harper's Ferry to the south. The first few days on trail were boring as I walked up and down forested hills without a view in sight.

However, once I crested Center Point Knob and crossed into the Cumberland Valley, the scenery changed. Forests were replaced by miles of cornfields and pasturelands. The sound of birds humming was replaced by automobiles and trains. Once I crossed the valley and climbed onto the next ridge, the scenery changed back to forest and I got my first glimpse at why hikers nickname the state "Rocksylvania." The trail was littered with rocks, but these weren't small individual rocks that could be moved or dug out, they were sharp rocks that had

Heading out onto the Appalachian Trail in Caledonia State Park.

been formed by eroding sandstone over thousands of years. Each step I took was a calculated decision because a wrong step would cause me to twist my ankle or slip and fall.

When I arrived in Duncannon and crossed over the Susquehanna River, I felt accomplished. I crossed my first major river and hiked almost 100 miles by now. On the far side of the river, the trail headed back up onto Pennsylvania's endless ridge and my journey continued through a maze of rocks. The rock fields also held dangers out of sight. Several times I passed a powerline crossing and was interrupted by the rattle of a venomous timber rattlesnake. But those dangers paled in comparison to the time when I found myself milliseconds away from stepping on a rattlesnake on Dan's Pulpit.

The rugged terrain wasn't always detrimental. Tucked away between the ridges were some of the most remote and beautiful places I have ever seen in Pennsylvania (and I lived there all my life). For about eight miles, the trail passed through an isolated valley situated between two ridges. For the first time in Pennsylvania, I found no signs or sounds of human activity, and the air and water were pristine. I knew this would be a premier fishing spot for brook trout and other cold-water fish, but because of its inaccessibility, there wasn't a soul in sight. The only traces of human inhabitation were the remains of an old coal mining settlement that was reclaimed by the forest. In that valley near Rausch Gap, I felt at home for the first time on the trail.

To reach the many trail towns in Pennsylvania, the trail dropped to a gap where a river or stream cut through the ridge. Some of the many gaps included: Swatara, Schuylkill, Lehigh, Wind, and Delaware Water Gaps. The trail towns were conveniently located just off the trail, and resupplying was easy. I also had the opportunity to meet some of my relatives along the trail, and I met my aunt at the Lehigh Gap. I spent a couple of days with her in Scranton, and once I got back on the trail, I experienced my first outbreak of DACS (Day After Civilization Syndrome). After sleeping on a comfy bed and eating whatever I desired, I felt that staying in civilization was a better way to spend my time than marching across the rocky terrain on Blue Mountain Ridge. So, a day after getting back on the trail, I started getting homesick, and I called my parents and told them that I felt like ending my hike then and there. They encouraged me to stick with it and see how life would fare in New Jersey. The following morning, I crossed into my next state.

New Jersey: Varied Terrain in a Varied World

"As long as we're not in Pennsylvania, I'm happy!"

- Leaky

For NOBOs, the state of New Jersey is a giant sigh of relief. Upon entering the state, the first climb up Kittany Mountain was different than how it was in Pennsylvania. Instead of a 1000' climb over a mile, the climb was several miles long. Hikers love New Jersey not only because it isn't Pennsylvania, but also because of its multivariate terrain. The trail follows Kittany Mountain for 40 miles, then crosses the Great Appalachian Valley with marshy areas full of boardwalks and wildlife preserves, followed by a few small mountains the trail ascends and descends. Although there isn't a lot of trail mileage in New Jersey, hikers are still rewarded with beautiful views along Kittany Range and at High Point State Park.

I felt empowered when I crossed the Delaware River, similar to how George Washington felt on Christmas Eve in 1776. He crossed the Delaware River with his army and attacked the British and Hessians in Trenton, New Jersey. My enemy was the trail, and I had already defeated Pennsylvania, and now I was on to the next state. I got my first glimpse at wild fruit along the trail, as I saw unripe green blueberries growing for the first time along the trail. They had a different taste than foods I had eaten recently, and the sour aftertaste was a satisfying change of pace. The weather was also pleasant, and it was warm every day with afternoon thunderstorms threatening. But somehow I was able to avoid being hit by the thunderstorms as they either fizzled out or struck north or south of my position.

Although there were still rocks littered along the trail, they were different than just a few miles south. During the last Ice Age, the southernmost extent of the glaciers was about to the Delaware Water Gap, and so the portion of trail in New Jersey was glaciated while Pennsylvania wasn't. This was some much-needed relief for hikers, and instead of the sharp, pointed rocks that were common throughout Pennsylvania, the mountains in New Jersey were rounded and contained flat rocks. That meant that I could walk much faster, and some of the summits were barren except for some grasses. When I reached High Point State Park, I met a former AT hiker at the summit and talked with him about the upcoming states. He told me that it was smooth sailing from New Jersey until I reached New Hampshire.

That was great news, and I thought about the upcoming trail as I trekked through the Great Appalachian Valley. Walking on the boardwalks through the swampy areas were enjoyable for my feet, but I knew how dangerous they were when moist. They became extremely slippery when wet, and if I took a wrong step, I may have ended up in the swamp after falling like Charlie Brown. When I hiked around Wallkill Preserve, I found myself being divebombed by several songbirds. Once I left them behind, I

The view from Pinwheel Vista on Wawayanda Mountain.

got to enjoy expansive views after climbing the "Stairway to Heaven" up Wawayanda Mountain.

New Jersey is known for a famous mining area, the Franklin and Sterling Hill Mines. There have been more than 350 different minerals discovered at the mines, which account for a whopping 10% of all minerals ever discovered. I saw the same mining spirit along the Appalachian Trail, when I passed the Green and Wawayanda Iron Mines. They were hematite mines excavated in the latter half of the nineteenth century, and I ventured off the trail to view their remains. After seeing the ruins, I ran across a baby black bear on my way back to the trail. Both New Jersey and New York are known for their rapidly growing bear populations, so I shouldn't have been surprised when I saw my first black bear out in the wild. I hiked to the shelter (which was a mile away) and relayed news of the bear sighting to everyone. We were cognizant about storing our food and by the next morning, I crossed into New York.

New York: New Yuck

"Hiking in New York reminds me every day why
I left the real world to hike the AT."

- Tarzan

The only state where the Appalachian Trail is close to a major metropolitan area is New York. From several points along the trail, I looked to the south and saw skyscrapers in downtown Manhattan. One night, I also spent a night at West Mountain Shelter, which was a whopping 0.6 miles off the trail (the farthest I ventured off trail for a shelter). When I woke up in the middle of the night, I put on my glasses and saw the skyscrapers all lit up. When I descended Bear Mountain, I emerged from the forest into a swarm of activity. It was unlike anything I had seen on the trail before, and after seeing all the people, I wanted to disappear back into the forest. Once I crossed the Bear Mountain Bridge over the Hudson River, my wish came true and I continued through the hills on the eastern side of the river as I approached Connecticut.

When I reached the first stream in New York, I knew I needed water, so I pulled out my filter and went about my usual procedure. But after filtering the water, it was still orange red. The locals said the color was derived from tannins in hemlock trees upstream, but I didn't buy that as the real reason. With my chemistry background, I knew that regardless of the hemlock forest density, there wouldn't be enough tannins to discolor the water as much as it was. Regardless, I continued and visited Greenwood Lake. After getting back on trail, my guidebook stated, "Despite the unimposing profile, rocks and abrupt ups and downs make this section challenging." Truer words had never been stated and I was absolutely exhausted after doing a 23-mile day followed by another 22-mile day in that unrelenting terrain.

On the first day, the trail crossed Harriman State Park. There, the trail passed through narrow valleys surrounded by daunting cliffs, and I was on edge. It was the perfect area to find a bear, and I grasped my dad's hunting knife as I walked down the trail in case anything jumped out at me. But, as I approached more populated areas, I was able to relax again. There, I suddenly emerged from the woods to a four-lane divided highway! It felt like I was playing the Frogger game when I crossed the Palisades Parkway with my pack on, although I knew how real it was. I dodged cars that were passing me going 70 mph.

The craziness ensued after descending Bear Mountain, where I was swarmed by a group of Boy Scouts that asked me a bunch of questions about hiking and my gear. I told them how I enjoyed hiking and how I felt after trekking more than 300 miles. After venturing into Fort Montgomery, I crossed the Bear Mountain Bridge. Unfortunately, there was road work on the bridge, and because they had the sidewalk and one of the lanes closed, I was forced to walk through the lanes of moving traffic to cross

A view of the Bear Mountain Bridge (and an Amtrak bridge) from Fort Montgomery.

the bridge. Once I reached the other side of the bridge, the amount of human activity was completely different than the previous ten miles. The footpath crossed through wooded land again, and after a few road crossings, I made it to Dennytown Road to camp for the night.

There, I set my tent up with another hiker named Chinook that I met earlier in the day when an unmarked car pulled up to the small gravel lot. A uniformed police officer got out and went over to two other hikers who were camped out next to their vehicles and spoke to them. I was close enough to discern what they were talking about. He asked if they were AT hikers and then he pointed at me and Chinook and told them, "Well, I see how beat up and dead they both look, so they must be hikers." Very true. The officer came over and made sure we were in fact AT hikers and not people looking for a campsite down the road at Clarence Fahnestock State Park. After he wished us luck and bade us adieu, we let out a collective sigh of relief because we weren't fined $250 for illegally camping.

That night, I didn't put my rainfly on my tent, instead I fell asleep gazing up at the stars. I tried to find something that would cheer myself up after my feet hurt like crazy and I was upset seeing all those people. I decided to lift my spirits by visiting some of the magnetite mines in the area. I collected a few samples from Thompson mine, but I knew they had to be small samples because I had to carry them for many more miles. Supposedly, the mines were excavated during the time of the Civil War, and the magnetite found there was melted into iron. From there, it was shipped downstream to the foundry in West Point where it was forged into cannonballs for the Union Army. In all the years of disuse since mining, the workings were filled with water, so I couldn't imagine how the mines looked all those years ago.

I continued hiking and once I reached RPH shelter, the trail changed. There were two major storms that I heard about when I started the trail: flooding on the Potomac River and severe storms in New York. Several areas along the trail were hit by damaging wind gusts. The trail looked like a war zone, all the pine and maple trees were snapped in half, and the winds were strong enough to lift entire oak trees and pull their root balls out of the ground. I met several volunteers who were cleaning up the last section of trail, a process that had been going on since the storm passed more than a month ago.

I met more of my relatives in nearby Beacon, NY, and after spending an afternoon with them and staying for the night with more my aunt and uncle, I got back on the trail near Nuclear Lake. The trail was smooth, and it wasn't long until I reached the Appalachian Trail Railroad station. I sat on the platform and ate lunch when I heard a train whistle off in the distance. A few minutes later, the train came into sight and blared its horn. The noise nearly made me drop my food, but it woke me up for the afternoon. Stunned and awake, I only had a few more miles until I reached Connecticut.

Connecticut: Short and Sweet

"You know, Lorax, you're so tall all you have to do to get through Connecticut is take four or five steps."

- Thumper

Connecticut was a fun and enjoyable state. Most hikers spend between two and four days in the state, and they experience low rolling hills along with the flattest portion of the AT, a handicap-accessible portion along the

Housatonic River. Doing big miles was easy statewide and there were plenty of places to resupply along the trail, making for a short and sweet state.

Hiking through Connecticut was a breeze, it was a quick two and a half days to cross from one side to the other. There were a few interesting sights, like Bulls Bridge, a covered bridge still in working condition. An hour later, I walked through the quaint town of Kent to resupply. From there, I arrived at the handicap-accessible trail. The trail was flat and followed the Housatonic River, and that was the fastest I hiked on the entire Appalachian Trail. Although the ground was flat and I made good time, my feet were wrecked by the time I reached Caesar's Brook Campsite. When I picked out my camp site for the night, I saw an interesting scene. Instead of being situated inside a privy, there was a toilet sitting in the middle of the woods. When I went to the bathroom

Hiking along the banks of the Housatonic River.

later, I saw it overlooked a view of Cornwall, CT. One of the other hikers put it perfectly when they said it was "Shitting with a view."

The next day I was walking along a road in nearby Falls Village when a car pulled up alongside me. The woman driving asked me a bunch of questions about my hike and gave me a bagel from Dunkin Donuts. It started sprinkling as we were talking, and she told me that if it was still raining when I reached Salisbury (where she lived), I was welcome to dry off and relax at her house. She wrote her phone number on a napkin, handed it to me, and then drove off. I wasn't planning on taking her up on the offer, as she was a stranger, and I didn't have much time. I had to be in Great Barrington (~40 miles away) in less than two days, but a few miles later when it started downpouring I had a change of heart. But when I searched in my pack for the napkin to text her, I couldn't find the napkin. I checked and rechecked my pack but still couldn't find it. When I arrived in Salisbury a few hours later (in the pouring rain), I wanted to take her up on the offer and ask to stay for the night, but without her number, the odds of seeing her were about zero.

Just a few miles from the Massachusetts border, I got my first true climb on the trail. This wasn't climbing out of a gap; it was just hiking straight up Lions Head. After staying at Riga Shelter, I reached the tallest peak in Connecticut, Bear Mountain, (although the tallest point in the state is along the side of another mountain that peaks in Massachusetts) and saw expansive views of the pastoral valleys below. After a steep descent into Sage's Ravine, I followed a narrow stream straddling the MA-CT border. I drank the crisp, clean mountain water, and looked at the virgin forest before continuing into Massachusetts.

Massachusetts: Gateway to the North

"Massachusetts is kind of just there: it's not as difficult as the last three states, but not as easy as the previous three states."

- Caveman

Massachusetts is a transition state on the trail, it is the first time that hikers ascend above 3000 feet for the first time since Shenandoah National Park in Virginia. However, the 600 miles the trail covered since then made a big difference for living conditions for plant life on the summit. This was the first time on the trail that I saw the tree growth was stunted, although they shrank more as I ventured northward. Massachusetts is a transition state, the Gateway to the North: continuing NOBO, hikers only have three states left on the trail, but the southern portion of the state looked different. It was similar to Connecticut and New York, with easily accessible trail towns and generally easy terrain. But in the northern section, hikers got to see expansive views from Mount Greylock and finish out the state in the Green Mountains.

Right after entering Massachusetts, I was greeted with beautiful views from Mount Race, and I assumed the same would be true for the nearby and slightly taller Mount Everett. However, I was disappointed when I discovered it was a wooded summit. My spirits were also dampened for a few miles near Jug End, when I came across a rocky section that reminded me of Pennsylvania (shudder). From there, the trail dipped into the mosquito-infested valley near Great Barrington. I passed the site of Shay's Rebellion, and instead of following the other hikers northward, I made my way back home to Pittsburgh. I quoted Arnold Schwarzenegger and told the other hikers, "I'll be back."

• • • • •

After enjoying some much-needed time at home eating more than my fair share of food and sleeping with a sense of security, I was back in Great Barrington a little over a week later. The trail wasn't too difficult, and I still had my trail legs, so I continued to make good miles through the rolling hills. I spent an evening at Upper Goose Pond Shelter, a shelter where a caretaker resided. Unfortunately, I couldn't stay for breakfast (pancakes and sausage) because I planned to hike as far as I could that day. After I weighed my pack on a hanging scale (a whopping 53 pounds), I left at sunrise and spent the day walking until my feet stopped working. The terrain was boring, but by the end of the day, I reached Dalton. After hiking the equivalent of a marathon, I set up camp, and the next morning, I saw the main challenge that Massachusetts threw at hikers, Mount Greylock.

I saw that there was bad weather in the forecast for the next two days, but it was a cloudless sky when I headed out in the morning. When I looked up, I wondered if I misread the forecast, but as I made the 2500-foot climb to the top, clouds rolled in and covered everything. The temperature also dropped and while it was in the low 80's and sunny at the base, a few hours later it was misting and windy in the 50's at the summit. The visibility was down to about twenty feet, and I could barely see people or the trail in front of me. I stopped to eat a quick snack at the summit, but I had to retreat below tree line because I felt my body temperature dropping. I hurriedly

Foggy summit of Mount Greylock.

moved on to Wilbur Clearing Shelter and spent a memorable night there in a thunderstorm. In the morning, I made my way down to North Adams. After crossing the Hoosic River, the skies opened up and the raindrops came falling down as I hiked towards the Vermont state line.

Vermont: Where It's Always Mud Season

"If I had a dollar for every puddle I've stepped in since I got into Vermont, I'd be a millionaire!"

- Zoltan

Vermont was hard to sum up. It is a unique state and unlike any other state on the trail or in the United States. Perhaps it was because Vermont was once a country or because of Ethan Allen and the Green Mountain Boys. I thought the Vermont section would be exciting (because of the Long Trail and Green Mountains), but it was less than I imagined. There were only a couple of viewpoints I found awe-inspiring, but I still enjoyed it. As another hiker put it, "The Long Trail is about 99% forest and 1% views." Additionally, every season is muddy in Vermont, and although I hiked there during a drier stretch, I stepped in more puddles than I wanted to.

The first day in Vermont was my least favorite day on the entire trail. The rain that started in North Adams, MA never stopped, and I trudged through the pouring rain all day. To add to my disappointment, I reached plenty of wooded summits during the day. It shouldn't have made a difference because I wouldn't have been able to see anything because of the fog. When I reached camp that night, I barely put up my tent in time before another batch of rain moved in. Things livened up a bit for me; I made to Bennington, the weather improved, and I met another hiker family. We climbed to Glastenbury Mountain and I finally got my first view from the state, atop a fire tower. We reached Stratton Mountain, or the "Birthplace of the Appalachian Trail," the next day and I celebrated because that was the halfway point of my section hike (550 miles down, 550 miles to go).

The weather took a dramatic turn that week, and it went from being cold and rainy to excruciatingly hot. The valley temperatures approached 100°, and the temperature reached between 90° and 95° up in the mountains. I ran out of water several times, and during one day in that span, I was so thirsty I drank twelve liters of water. When I climbed out of the Clarendon Gorge, I scrambled up a steep section that was exposed and full of car-sized boulders. After spending ten minutes climbing that section in the sweltering heat, I collapsed onto the ground at the top. Another hiker came by, saw me lying face-down on the ground, and asked if I was okay. All I could do was mutter something and give him a feeble thumbs-up. It took another twenty minutes for me to get up off the ground, and after gathering the strength to carry on, I tried hiking shirtless. After a tenth of a mile, I felt my shoulders were already starting to chafe and I was probably getting sunburnt, so I put my shirt back on and stumbled down the trail.

The next mountain I climbed was Killington, and thankfully the trail up the four-thousand footer was fairly smooth and I cruised until I reached the side trail to the summit. After scaling the trail to the summit, I was disappointed by the swirling clouds that obscured my view from the top. Once I reached the bottom, I visited Rutland. From there, the Appalachian Trail split off from the Long Trail and headed due east. All that remained between me and New Hampshire was forty miles of rolling hills. They were fairly difficult, and although I knocked them out in just two days, those miles took a toll on my legs. Additionally, there were only a few views, so I found myself listening

Small pastoral valleys in the eastern part of Vermont.

to music to force myself forward. When I reached West Hartford, I saw my first SOBO hiker. From then on, I saw between five and ten SOBO's every day as part of "The Convergence." I saw SOBO's long after I crossed the Connecticut River into New Hampshire.

New Hampshire: Welcome to the Whites

"If these views weren't this beautiful, I wouldn't have made it through the Whites."

- Single Gear

If you were to ask anybody (not just a hiker) what the first thing that came to their mind was when talking about New Hampshire, most people would say the White Mountains. Just as the Green Mountains are synonymous with Vermont, the Whites are known for New Hampshire. And despite how rugged they were, they were home to some of the most spectacular sights along the trail. The view from Mount Lafayette back over Franconia Ridge is the second-most photographed spot on the trail (McAfee Knob in Virginia is the most photographed), and it is easy to see why this portion of the trail is one of the most common day hiking locations.

Just like that, after I crossed the Connecticut River, I was in my penultimate state. I walked around Dartmouth College in Hanover then I continued through fragmented pieces of the White Mountain National Forest. When I hiked up my first mountain, it had a different feeling. There was a chill in the air, and I could see nothing but wilderness from Moose Mountain. I was stunned at the views from Smarts Mountain and Mount Cube, and there I got my first glimpse of Mount Moosilauke. The majestic summit rose above all the and the peak was just below cloud level.

Before reaching the base, I still had to traverse a huge valley, and after I met Omelette Karl, I made it to the mountain. The 4000-foot climb to the summit was the first time I had a steep hike with that kind of elevation difference, so I tried something different. Instead of listening to music, I decided to sing "99 Bottles of Beer on the Wall" out loud the entire way to the top. After finishing off my 198th bottle of beer, I was just about at the summit. The views were panoramic and spectacular, and that was also my first experience in the White Mountains. The trail down Mount Moosilauke followed a cascading stream and was exceptionally steep. When I saw slackpackers I knew headed to the peak, I muttered something in disgust as they passed me. The next days were no exception, and I found myself climbing straight up and then right back down the next side of the mountain, but each of the views were to die for. I reached the first White Mountain Hut at Lonesome Lake, and I was delighted when they told me I could fill up my water bottles at a faucet inside and I didn't need to filter it.

I resupplied in Lincoln and spent the night at a stealth spot in my tent on the side of Franconia Ridge. That night, a thunderstorm blew through, and I heard lightning striking off the top of the ridge. When I was on top of the ridge in the morning, the clouds had mostly passed, and I was left with a jaw-dropping view of Franconia Ridge. The picture that I took that morning is shown on the front cover of this book. The rocky trail continued through the rugged terrain, and I slept near the summit of South Twin Mountain. I woke up to temperatures in the upper 30's, which was a brutal reminder that although it was mid-July, the area was still dangerous.

After traversing into and out of Crawford Notch, I felt a twinge in my groin, and feared the worst. I first injured my groin playing collegiate basketball a few years before, and I worried that I wouldn't be able to continue hiking as I limped two miles to my camp site. Fortunately, I felt better the next day, and it was just in time because that day I had to cross the Presidential Range. After I ate a pound of leftover pancakes at the Lake of the Clouds Hut, I set out on the mile-long climb to the summit of Mount Washington. The pancakes didn't sit well in my stomach, but I reached the top without them coming up. Mount Washington holds the record for the highest wind speed on

A picture of me from the summit of Mount Washington, the highest point on my section of the Appalachian Trail.

Earth, but when I arrived at the summit, the temperature was 48° with a measly 8 mph wind.

The tourists there stared at me the way a disappointed parent looks at their child. They shook their heads at me and walked away. I figured they were probably the same people that purchased a bumper sticker saying, "My

Car Climbed Mount Washington" and felt proud of their accomplishment. The clouds started looking menacing, so I got off the summit as quickly as possible, but I was still trapped in a 20 mile stretch above tree line. When I arrived at Madison Hut, I was permitted to do a Work-for-Stay (WFS) by the caretakers with a couple of other hikers. That night, I feasted on real food and slept on the floor of a heated building in my sleeping bag, so I couldn't complain about anything.

In the morning, I descended Mount Madison in the rain and clambered over the Wildcat mountains. I watched a wedding ceremony in the rain on Wildcat Mountain Peak D, then I headed over Carter Dome and the remaining mountains until I reached Gorham. On my way out of Gorham, I visited the Mascot Mine and took a side trail to Mount Hayes to reconnect with the Appalachian Trail. The progress on this section was even slower than in the Whites, and once I set my tent up at Gentian Pond Shelter, I saw a moose wading in the pond. That was a pleasant ending to New Hampshire, and I crossed the border into Maine the next morning.

Maine: The Way Life Should Be

"If you can't stand the pain,
And aren't willing to walk in the rain,
Then you'll never make it to Maine."

- Hiking Proverb

Maine is the ultimate goal for just about every NOBO hiker on the trail. But despite the plethora of hikers who think they have what it takes to make it to Maine, a majority fall short. In a typical year, only about a quarter of hikers who set out from Springer Mountain with the goal of reaching Katahdin end up making it. I can't imagine hiking all the way to Maine and having to quit so close to the end. The feeling would kill me, so it was important to be cautious in Maine. However, there were plenty of reasons Maine isn't "The Way Life Should Be" for a hiker, because the temperature is cooler, the terrain is extremely rough (especially in southern Maine), and the resupply points are few and far-between. Maine's weather also plays a key role in a hike because the state is known for day-long rains, which can greatly slow your pace and make you miserable. Additionally, snow starts falling in the mountains in later October, and Baxter State Park closes on October 15th, (if not earlier). Life in the forest is also more difficult in Maine, as the trees grow much closer together and attain lesser heights than everywhere else.

For me, Maine started out with a bang. I woke up to temperatures at Carlo Col Shelter in the upper 30's, and a few miles later I found myself on Goose Eye Mountain, but it was different. The winds were howling with gusts 40 to 50 mph, but more impressively, it was snowing (on July 18th)! As I trudged across the north peak in my typical hiking attire (shorts and a t-shirt), my body froze in the ice-cold wind as snowflakes coated my glasses. The winds were strong enough that they blew my rain cover off my pack, but I was lucky enough to grab it before it flew off the summit. The five minutes I spent above tree line felt like an eternity, and when I emerged from the clouds a mile later, I got a chance to look ahead at my next task: the Mahoosuc Notch.

Depending on the hiker you ask, the Mahoosuc Notch is either the hardest or most fun-filled mile on the entire Appalachian Trail. For a 1.1-mile stretch, the trail passes between overhanging cliffs through a giant boulder field. In there, hikers must pass over, around, and under boulders to emerge on the other side. I worried for days about not being able to make it across the Notch, and I even debated hiking twelve miles for a detour to get around that section of trail. However, I took my time and slowly crossed it in 2:13, a respectable time considering my pace as I clambered in the rocks. Once it was over, I felt a huge sense of accomplishment and as I enjoyed a victory lunch on the other side, a bird pooped on my arm! After cleaning that up, I realized I had a steep climb up Mahoosuc Arm. Another saying on the trail goes, "The Notch kicks you in the crotch, but the Arm does the harm." By the time I made it to the top of Mahoosuc Arm and hiked to Old Speck Mountain, I had quite an exciting first day in Maine.

I wish I could say the trail got easier, but it wasn't. Progress was slow and steady until I reached Rangeley, where the trail was "flatter," but after only a few easy miles there, I entered the four-thousand footers in Maine. Before I knew it, I hiked up Saddleback (4121'), The Horn (4042'), Mount Spaulding (4010'), South Crocker (4050'), Crocker Mountain (4228'), along with West (4145') and Avery Peak (4090') in the Bigelows. In this mountainous stretch, the tree growth was much thicker, and the Balsam Fir trees occluded views from some of the summits and I couldn't even see a few feet off the trail. The forest looked identical everywhere I looked, and I was alert to the disorienting nature of the forest, which was dangerous because how remote the area was. On July 22, 2013, a hiker named Inchworm got lost after heading out from Poplar Ridge Shelter, and despite the largest manhunt in Maine history, she wasn't found. It wasn't until more than two years later when a forester stumbled upon her camp. I said a prayer for her when I passed the shelter and I asked for safe passage, because I was at Poplar Ridge Shelter on...July 22nd!

After I crossed the Bigelows, I had conquered almost all the large mountains in Maine, and the trail got much smoother. But the next challenge that I faced were stream crossings. Before hiking the Appalachian Trail, I had never forded a river, and picturing myself wading across a river with my pack didn't seem like a good idea. To make matters worse, the weather took a turn for the worst after I passed Rangeley, and I got rained on for eight straight days. With the added runoff, the streams were all swollen, which made my crossings sketchier than they were for other hikers. When I reached the Hundred Mile Wilderness, I was met by two crossings on my first day that were knee and waist deep with rushing water. I still have nightmares about crossing Big Wilson and Little Wilson Streams. I faced upstream and slowly inched across the chilly waters as my hiking poles violently shook from the force of the water.

But like all things, the water level returned to normal as the weather improved. My last ford was eighty miles from Katahdin, and I flew through the flatter (ford-free) half of the Hundred Mile Wilderness. Although I emerged a day earlier than expected, I ran out of food and I went to bed hungry the night before emerging from the woods. To make matters worse, my phone stopped charging, and I couldn't take any pictures for a fifty mile stretch until I met Coyote at Abol Bridge. From there, I made my way into Baxter State Park and spent one final night at The Birches. I woke up bright and early on August 4th in the rain as I hiked up Hunt Trail. Once I arrived at The Tablelands, I was shrouded by clouds as sheets of rain soaked me. Besides a light rain jacket, I had left all my rain gear at the foot of the mountain, so I was shivering and sopping wet when I reached the summit. I was the first person to summit Katahdin that day, and after crying tears of joy and celebrating at the summit sign, I got a picture of myself with the Appalachian Trail northern terminus sign when a few other hikers arrived.

The northern terminus of the Appalachian Trail at the summit of Mount Katahdin.

AT Trail Towns

Nestled in the valleys surrounding the Appalachian Trail are some of the most beautiful towns in the United States. I had the opportunity to visit plenty of them on my section hike, and each town had its own unique style. I was excited to see the architecture and town layout, and since I had never seen or heard of (except Kent) them, I was fully immersed in the towns as I walked down the main street of each town. Many of these towns had a rapidly declining population, and attracting young people was difficult in these areas because there were no high-paying jobs in these small, rural towns. But regardless, I got to experience a side of America I had never seen before, and I always looked forward to seeing the next trail town and meeting the locals in the next town every few days.

Duncannon, PA – 1042.6 miles to Katahdin

There I was, poised to enter my first trail town after hiking more than seventy miles. Over the course of my first few days on trail, I already developed hiker stench, so when I reached Mutzabaugh's Market and got a good whiff of myself, I almost dry heaved. Luckily, the shoppers were used to hikers passing through, but I still felt terrible for anyone stuck in the same aisle as me. It was a strange feeling shopping for myself, as I knew I could get whatever I desired, as long as it lasted the next few days. I grabbed a bunch of food, checked out, then sat outside the store huddled against the wall where I ate some fresh fruit I purchased. I felt like a homeless person (and in a lot of ways I was) for the first time in my life as I sat on the ground with all my possessions leaning against me. Passersby stared at me and shook their heads disapprovingly, but that was a feeling I grew accustomed to over the next few months.

Most other hikers wanted to stay at the Doyle Hotel, but I knew it was only 2:30 in the afternoon and I had plenty of strength left, so I continued. I approached the Juniata and Susquehanna River crossing, and I saw police officers redirecting traffic to the next bridge over the river, which was eleven miles to the south. Thankfully, I didn't have to follow the detour, and when I got onto the bridge, I saw a semi-tractor trailer was flipped on its side after rounding a curve going too fast. After a six hour cleanup, the crews were about to reopen the bridge.

Hamburg/Port Clinton, PA – 972.0 miles to Katahdin

After the trail steeply descended from Blue Mountain into the Schuylkill Gap, I arrived in Port Clinton. I was hiking with two others, and the first thing that Pacemaker and Beachbum did when they got into town was went straight to the tavern. There, they followed their ritual and ordered a couple of beers, like they did at every trail town they had passed. Aside from the fact that I prefer wine over beer, I knew it was costly to buy a couple of drinks at every town I visited along the trail (like some hikers do). To do a little bit of math (I am an engineer after all), an average cost of drinking at each town was about $10-15, and since I visited 20 different trail towns on the Appalachian Trail, that puts my alcohol tab between $200 and $300. That was about a quarter of the total amount I spent on food for the entire trail, so it's easy to see how alcohol can eat into your budget for a trip.

Instead of going with them to the bar, I went into Hamburg, which is known for having the largest Cabela's store in the world. If you enjoy the great outdoors, this store is a must-see, with over 250,000 ft^2 of space and a huge selection of gear. They also offered free rides into town for Appalachian Trail hikers. I called them and asked for a ride, and fifteen minutes later, they picked me up and dropped me off at the Cabela's. I spent an hour grazing through the store looking at all their gear while simultaneously trying to avoid exposing everyone to my unpleasant smell got worse over the last few days.

After shopping at Cabela's and Walmart, I headed back to Port Clinton for the night. Although Hamburg and Port Clinton are separated by less than two miles, there is a half-mile long bridge that separates them with no sidewalk or shoulder, which meant I had to find another way across the valley. I pulled out my trail guide and saw there was a rail trail (Schuylkill River Trail) that passed nearby, and when I got onto the trail, I was surprised at how small the path alongside the railroad tracks was. The sun was setting, so I flipped on my headlights as I walked the three miles back. Suddenly, my path was illuminated by something much brighter than my headlight!

I whipped around and saw a freight train coming right at me. I sprinted off the tracks and ran into the woods. The train approached and blared its horn as it neared me, as if the conductor knew I was nearby. The train passed by without stopping, and once it was out of sight I emerged from the woods and continued following the tracks towards Port Clinton. After crossing a narrow bridge over a large creek, I entered a loading yard and ran to the parking lot to make it seem like I was a worker. After breathing a sigh of relief, I walked to the pavilion in town, where hikers were permitted to spend the night. I got a good night of sleep along with the other fifteen hikers that were there, and in the morning, I found out that I wasn't on the rail trail. Instead, I was on the Reading and Northern Railroad, oops! I got up on the foggy morning, ate a loaf of Italian bread, then continued hiking.

Wind Gap, PA – 911.7 miles to Katahdin

Wind Gap was a good distance off the trail, and I had to get to the Giant grocery store, which was 2.5 miles away. I tried hitching for a minute, until I remembered that people in Pennsylvania don't pick up hitchhikers from the side of the road. So, I made the long walk into town; and my feet, which were already tired and very sore, weren't thrilled about walking all the way there. I got to Giant, purchased my food, then went to a nearby Burger King. I grabbed something to eat, then I realized how far behind schedule I was for the day. Begrudgingly, I headed back to the trail. Walking back to the trail was difficult with the additional twenty pounds of food. Thankfully, after walking a mile back, an elderly couple stopped and gave me a ride back to the trail.

Unionville, NY – 844.7 miles to Katahdin

There is a joke among hikers on the Appalachian Trail that the best trail town in New Jersey is Unionville, New York. You read that correctly! As a hiker, it makes sense because there are no decent trail towns in New Jersey. Additionally, Unionville is located a stone's throw from New Jersey. When I walked into town, I was shocked at how small the town was. The previous trail towns I had visited were much bigger and more developed, and here I was in a quaint little village. I was also amazed at the hospitality of the locals, and as I walked down the main street in town, multiple people were out on their front porches and waved to me. They asked me some questions about my journey, and after fielding them, I went to the general store and reserved a camping spot in the town park that night.

The next spot I visited was Wit's End Tavern, which was known in the AT hiking community (and was mentioned in my trail guide) for their excellent ribs. I followed their suggestion and I ordered a full slab of ribs and a pint of root beer. That was the most delicious meal that my taste buds remembered, and I took my time with the ribs. I ate them slowly and enjoyed every bite. In the middle of dinner, I met two middle-aged female hikers (Puddles and Thumper) who were just about finished with their food. After we finished eating, we went to Annabele's Pizza, and got some ice cream.

We sat on the porch and talked with more of the townsfolk about our difficulties on the trail and why we enjoyed hiking enough to go on a crazy adventure like this. As hiker midnight approached, the three of us headed to the town park and set up our tents in a grassy spot between the flower garden and basketball court. After getting a sound night of sleep, I awoke to the sound of people walking by on the main street, and I packed my life back up and I headed onward.

Greenwood Lake, NY – 819.9 miles to Katahdin

I was exhausted and tired when I crossed into New York (this time for real), and in no time, I scrambled off the ridge on Valley Vista Trail into Greenwood Lake. It was perfect timing because I only had a few snacks left because I only got a few items in Unionville. First, I went to Country Grocery, where I bought most of my food. I sat outside on a bench and ate a mango as I saw storm clouds brewing in the sky. After I headed out, I walked down the street to Cumberland Farms, where I bought a few more things. I also left the bathroom air as extremely toxic (I think you know what I mean) on my way out. I visited the post office next, and when I found that my shoes were not there (which was a whole different story), I walked two miles along the side of the road to get back to the trail.

There was a hot dog stand set up at the trailhead that I thought was open until 3:00. So, when I was in town and saw it was 2:45, I knew I wasn't going to make it, so I took my time getting back on the trail. I arrived there at 3:34, but as it turned out, the stand was open until 3:30 and I just missed him! So, instead of drowning my sorrows with hot dogs, I walked down the road to Bellvale Farms, and ate homemade ice cream. The skies were clear by now, as I ate my ice cream on a picnic table, I peered down into the valley below.

Fort Montgomery, NY – 786.0 miles to Katahdin

The story of Fort Montgomery is entirely tied to my shoes (get it?), and because of how disappointed I was, I didn't enjoy Fort Montgomery at all. When I descended Bear Mountain, the AT passed through the Trailside Museum and Zoo, but I got there thirty minutes before the zoo opened, so I took the weed-infested bypass around the zoo. I walked across a footbridge and saw some of the exhibits of the Revolutionary War Fort Montgomery. When I finished climbing up the hill, I found myself in an unfamiliar location. I was walking by the side of the road in a neighborhood full of elegant mansions with fine-trimmed yards. There were several homeowners who were out collecting their garbage cans from the street, and they scoffed at me when they saw how I looked.

I put up with their stares, and made it to the Post Office, where my shoes were still MIA. I called the company and cried in the parking lot because of how badly my feet were hurting, then I started to walk back to the Bear Mountain Bridge. When I checked the Maps app on my iPhone, I saw there was a McDonalds along the way, so I thought I would stop in and drink a large sweet tea to cheer myself up. When I reached the spot where it said there was a McDonalds, I looked around and only saw a residential house. It didn't look like there was ever a McDonalds there, and my mood sank even lower. After all of that disappointment, I crossed the Hudson River and continued northwards.

Kent, CT – 722.5 miles to Katahdin

The only trail town that I had heard of before learning about the Appalachian Trail was Kent. And the only reason I remembered it was because I knew someone from there who went to Seton Hill University with me. Who could have imagined I knew someone from that tiny town of less than 3,000 situated more than ten hours from school? Anyways, Kent was the quaint little town I pictured it would be, a settlement along the Housatonic River tucked amongst the rolling hills of Connecticut.

After walking about a mile into town, my first order of business was to rustle up some grub for the next upcoming days. Once I bought the food from the Davis IGA, I walked to the town square and laid down in the shade with six other hikers, and had a "fruit fiesta." My lunch consisted of: one pound of watermelon, one pound of strawberries, two pounds of applesauce, two yogurt containers, and one quart of root beer. I couldn't believe I ate it all, and afterwards I went looking for an ATM. To get to it, I walked all the way back to the southern end of town (the side the trail was on), but I found the ATM was out of money! And so that meant that I had to walk back to the northern side of town to use another ATM. As if I wasn't sick of walking already, I got the money and had to walk back across town to the trail, and in the middle of an already long day, I added an extra three miles to my legs.

Great Barrington, MA – 669.2 miles to Katahdin

When I reached Route 7, which led into Great Barrington, I was relieved that I was finally out of the woods, but I was also stressed about other things. I knew I had to find a place to stay in town for the night but more importantly I had to plan for a way to reach Pittsfield by the following afternoon. I got about twenty minutes into the three mile road walk, when a trail angel offered me a ride into town. She was extremely helpful and dropped me off at the Berkshire South Regional Community Center. At the community center, hikers were welcome to sleep on the tent pads in the woods along their nature trails. I went in, reserved my site, then called Four Brothers Pizza to order a pizza for dinner.

After I ordered the pizza, I went to Price Chopper and bought myself a two liter bottle of grape soda, and by the time I walked to the pizza place, they had the pizza ready for me. I walked back to the community center with a two liter in one hand and the pizza box in the other. I passed two people who looked homeless and when they passed me, they both told me about how good the authentic Greek pizza was. When I made it back to the community center, I sat under a gazebo and settled in for a feast. I ate 10 of the 12 slices of the 16" pepperoni-sausage-bacon 2XL pizza, and I was stuffed by the time I was done. After ditching the pizza box, I hung my food bag and retreated to my tent in the drizzle that just began. That night, I slept terribly, I was so hot (probably because my body was metabolizing two pounds of pizza), and to make matters worse, I ran out of water in the middle of the night. There weren't any water sources nearby, so as a last resort, I drank the remaining grape soda as a substitute. The added sugar and caffeine only made my sleep more sporadic.

I survived the night and "slept in" until 8:30. I paid $7 to go into the community center, where I filled up my water bottles, took a shower, and went swimming. So, after taking a twenty minute initial shower, I swam in the pool. I didn't have swimming trunks with me, so I dived right in with my hiking shorts. Unfortunately, a group of elderly people reserved most of the pool for their workout, but I was still able to swim and relax in the swimming lanes for an hour, which was followed by yet another long shower. I grabbed my pack, walked to McDonalds, and caught up with the other hikers I saw in Kent a few days ago. I told them that I was leaving the trail to go home and see my family. And I also told them that I wasn't sure if I would be back out on the AT in a few weeks or not. After I ate my fair share of food, I caught a bus outside of Price Chopper that took me into Pittsfield, MA. From there, I journeyed by train to Rochester, NY and met up with some family friends. They were gracious enough to drive me all the way back to Pittsburgh, PA the following day for my younger brother's graduation party.

Dalton, MA – 621.1 miles to Katahdin

I entered Dalton at the end of a very long day on the trail. That was the day where I hiked a marathon, so I was excited to get off my feet and to relax. Perhaps it was my limited food supply (and thus lower pack weight) that helped propel me to such a long day, but either way, the trail passed directly through town. I resupplied at the Cumberland Farms and Citgo convenience stores since there was no grocery store in town. I went to Angelina's Subs and ordered a buffalo chicken sub. It was supposed to help me power through the remaining few miles of the day, but I was disappointed when I got the sub. I opened the sub and saw it was merely a few chicken strips with some buffalo sauce tossed on them. I swallowed my tongue, after all it was still better than trail food, and I shoveled it down and continued out of town. I got to catch a few minutes of a little league baseball game on the far side of town as the sun crept lower in the sky.

Bennington, VT – 579.2 miles to Katahdin

Bennington was the first trail town I came across that was a substantial distance from the trail. The town center was 5.3 miles from the trail, and I needed to go an additional 1.8 miles to reach Walmart. I made the decision to hitchhike into town, and it felt strange hitchhiking for the first time in my life. I didn't know what to expect when I came off that Green Mountain pass onto Rt. 9. Luckily the road was wide and there was a decent flow of cars, but each time a car passed and I held out my thumb, nobody bothered to pull over. I walked further and further off the mountain, and I still had no luck getting a hitch. By now, it was 11:00 and it was in the mid-80's, so I was sweating pretty badly after walking for an hour. After being passed by more than 200 cars, somebody finally pulled over and let me in. The driver was a microbiologist traveling back from a conference in Boston. He gave me a lift to Walmart, where I bought all my provisions for the next leg of my journey. I told myself that never again would I wait that long for a ride into town, and thankfully that was the longest I waited for a hitch on the whole trek.

After stuffing all the food into my pack in the Walmart parking lot (with several onlookers amusingly watching), I walked towards town to a

McDonalds to get some grub. I bought a bunch of food, and I recharged my batteries (literally and figuratively) while I ate. I didn't want to have to rely on a hitch back to the trail, so I searched for an alternate way to get to the trail. I saw in my guidebook that there was a bus that took hikers back to the trailhead for a few dollars, so I decided to do that. I made the 1.5-mile walk to the Green Mountain Express terminal in town, and I got a ride back to the trailhead that was totally worth the $3 I paid for it. I was finally back on the trail, just two hours later than I anticipated.

Rutland, VT – 489.0 miles to Katahdin

Because of my fiasco getting into Bennington, I researched the best way to get into Rutland without having to rely on a hitch. Once again, the town was 8.5 miles from the trail, but now I knew there was a bus that took hikers into town and where I could catch it. So, I planned my day around catching the hourly bus at 3:34. When I arrived at the Inn at Long Trail at 3:18, I assumed I had a few minutes to catch my breath, but as it turned out, the bus pulled into the parking lot right whenever I arrived. I raced to the bus like a madman and made it on before it departed, which it did at 3:22, 12 minutes before it was scheduled to. It rolled into the bus station in downtown Rutland, and I first purchased more supplies at Walmart. A few hours ago, I heard from another hiker about the hospitality of the Yellow Deli, a hiker-friendly hostel run by a Twelve Tribes spiritual community. The hiker said I could shower and spend the night for free. I don't know about you, but anything free sounds great to me! So, I went in, reserved my bunk, and took a shower for the first time in more than two weeks.

After getting cleaned up and changing into town clothes, I went to the Rutland Free Library. I had some electronic paperwork that I needed to complete on an actual computer (and not on my iPhone), so they gave me an hour of internet access. I needed every minute to finish stuff I needed to get done, especially considering graduate school started in a month and a half. After I ate dinner at Wendys, I went to Price Chopper and bought myself half of a watermelon and a two liter of Brisk iced tea. I walked across the street and sat on a bench. There, I enjoyed the food and watched the sun set over the horizon.

I reached the hostel just in time for curfew. I threw in a load of laundry and spent some time with other hikers as we played the Appalachian Trail board game. Thanks to my extensive background in forestry and geography, I swept each game we played. After getting tired of winning (and my laundry finished), I hit the hay, but not before I went out on the roof and watched some fireworks go off (it was July 3rd).

I got up early in the morning to help prepare breakfast for the hikers and customers. I did that as my way of thanking them for allowing me to stay the night. My job was to slice up a bunch of fruit (the hikers called me the "Fruit Ninja"), and I prepared several different types of bread for customers. When it was time to eat, we had eggs with sausage, peppers, and onions along with rice with tomatoes. To drink, they made us a type of tea called maté. It was time to catch the bus after breakfast, and I collected my belongings and walked a block to the bus station, where I caught a ride back to the trail near Killington ski resort.

Hanover, NH – 442.1 miles to Katahdin

When I crossed the bridge over the Connecticut River that separates Norwich, VT and Hanover, NH, it really started to hit me that I was approaching the conclusion of my hike. Although I was slightly more than halfway done with the section, I had the two hardest, yet most rewarding states in front of me. Hanover is known by most people not for an Appalachian Trail town, but as the college town for Dartmouth College. I had a little bit of extra time to stroll around Dartmouth College, and I spent thirty minutes touring some of the buildings and the architecture.

I met one of my friends from Maine (who happened to be in a nearby town for the weekend), and we went to a restaurant in town called the Skinny Pancake. I ordered a Rueben and to my surprise, there was no corned beef on it. Instead, it had some other type of meat that tasted very different, and to this day I still don't know what was on that sandwich. Anyways, once I finished eating, I said goodbye to her and headed to the co-op store in town to purchase more food for the next leg of the journey. As I checked out, the cashier told me that he was headed up to Maine to hike the Hundred Mile Wilderness in 3 weeks and there was a chance I might see him up there. I knew it would be a long shot for me to get there in that time frame (it turned out to be about 4.5 weeks). And after I checked out, I resumed hiking and the trail disappeared behind the Dartmouth softball field. I was officially in the White Mountain National Forest.

Lincoln, NH – 373.1 miles to Katahdin

Hiking in the White Mountains was tough, and I ended up burning more calories (and thus eating more food) than I had previously, so I barely had enough food to reach Lincoln. There were two roads that led into town, Interstate 93 and Route 3, a highway and a two-lane road, but I had to hitchhike on the lesser traveled two-lane road. After I walked for an hour, local finally picked me up. He told me everything I could possibly know about Lincoln and why he loved the town so much. He told me that they get about ten weeks of summer year-round and that it was already week six. It seemed strange that the weather would already be changing to fall in about a month (since it was mid-July). He drove me into town and dropped me off at Price Chopper, where I picked up all my food for the next 80 miles of rough, White Mountain terrain.

I barely was able to fit all the food into my pack, but when I did, I walked down the main street to a McDonalds. There, I ordered food and charged my batteries, while I planned the upcoming days. I was particularly disappointed when I discovered that their sweet tea dispenser was filled with unsweetened tea. I had been waiting for days to drink some sweet tea, and yet there I was. I talked with a couple of the locals about the different trail sections ahead, then I began to road walk and search for a hitch back to the trailhead. I got about half of a mile on Route 3 when I was picked up by somebody. He was hauling some hemlock logs to his sawmill in the notch, and he gave me a ride to the Flume Visitor Center in Franconia Notch.

Gorham, NH – 298.3 miles to Katahdin

When I descended into Pinkham Notch (at the base of Mount Washington), I knew I had maybe a day's worth of food left, but nonetheless I decided to take on the Wildcats. I decided to go into Gorham a day later once I reached the other side of the mountain range. After a miserable day on the trail being drenched in rain, I took a detour once I arrived at Mt. Moriah. Instead of following the Appalachian Trail to the Androscoggin River, I blue blazed it on the Carter Moriah Trail into Gorham. That turned out to be a great decision, as the well-maintained steady downhill section of the trail was easy to walk on and the trail ended right on the outskirts of Gorham.

Since they were out of sweet iced tea at the Lincoln McDonalds, I wanted to have some when I reached the McDonalds in Gorham. However, I got there and saw the building was under construction, so I decided to "Have it My Own Way" and I went to Burger King across the street. I was spent a couple of hours there as I charged my power banks and my head, plus I ordered some ice cream in honor of National Ice Cream Day. Afterwards, I walked down the street and passed Dynasty Buffet, an all-you-can-eat Chinese buffet where a bunch of other hikers were headed that night, but I kept walking north to Walmart. It turned out that several of the hikers who stopped at the buffet got sick that night, either from the food or eating too much of it, which forced them to take several zeros afterwards.

It was a mile to walk to Walmart, and just after the road transitioned into a divided highway, a car pulled off the road in front of me and asked if I needed a ride. I accepted and they took me to Walmart. Along the way, they asked where I planned to stay for the night. By now, it was 7:30 and the sun was setting in a little less than hour, so I told them I was planning to head back to the trail and camp alongside the road. They told me that wasn't acceptable and that I could spend the night with them. They told me I was welcome to sleep on their couch and take a hot shower (which I desperately needed – and no, when it rained, that didn't count as a shower!). So, they dropped me off at Walmart, and when I finished, I sent them a text and they came and picked me up.

As it turns out, both of them hiked sections of the Appalachian Trail, and Baseweight thru-hiked the entire trail several years ago. When she passed through, she fell in love with the area and after finishing the trail, she moved to the Androscoggin River Valley and started working there. When we arrived in Berlin (the next town over from Gorham), I noticed over her doorway she had a piece of tree bark with a white blaze on it. She told me that it reminded her of how the trail led her to this tiny town tucked away in the White Mountains. I showered, threw in my laundry, and headed to bed. When I woke up in the morning, I ate some of the food I bought them for breakfast and Baseweight drove me down the road to a different trailhead.

I went with a different plan this time, and I asked to be dropped off by an abandoned railroad bridge. After walking with a hunchback to duck under for the four-foot clearance the bridge had over the Androscoggin River, I walked through back trails until I reached the remains of the Mascot Mine. I read about the mine the night before, and I learned it used to be a lead and silver mine, but all that remained was a giant pile of mine tailings. I dug through them and found some pieces of malachite and chalcopyrite. After I finished digging with my bare hands, I followed a side trail that met back up with the Appalachian Trail on Mount Hayes and I was on my way into Maine.

Andover, ME – 256.9 miles to Katahdin

The last few miles of New Hampshire and the first forty miles in Maine are considered the most difficult section on the entire Appalachian Trail, so I was excited when I emerged victorious from the woods. And I wasn't able to think of a better way to celebrate than by doing an eight mile road walk into town! The road leading into Andover (East B Hill Road) was a mere dirt backroad, and in my first hour walking into town, I didn't see a single car. About two hours into walking, a small school bus drove in my direction, and stopped alongside me. The driver stopped and asked if I wanted a ride into town. As it turned out, the driver was Yukon, the owner of the new Human Nature Hostel in Andover, which just opened that year. As we drove to the trailhead, he asked if I was going to spend the night in Andover. I told him that I only planned to spend an hour in town, but if I changed my mind, I would let him know. We pulled up to the trailhead and didn't see any hikers there, so he turned the bus around, and we made our way into town.

My first objective, like always, was to resupply. Because Andover was such a small town, my only option for food was at the overpriced Andover General Store. I got my rations and sat outside on the porch as I let my legs relax. For once, I wasn't eating anything. No, I was waiting another thirty minutes for the only restaurant in town to open, the Little Red Hen. It was a restaurant that served all-you-can-eat food most days of the week, and today (Thursday), was all-you-can-eat Mexican food.

I saved up room in my stomach all day, and when the restaurant opened, I was one of the first people inside. By the time the I finished eating, I devoured four platters full of Mexican goodness. Looking back at that dinner, I probably consumed between 4,000 and 5,000 calories in just that one sitting. I was stuffed, but unfortunately, I still had to make it back to the trail. After walking for about fifteen minutes, a couple from Andover kindly gave me a ride to the trailhead, which I reached as the sun set. The next day, I had another opportunity to hitchhike into Andover, and I learned that the Little Red Hen was having prime rib that night, but despite the temptations that I felt, I managed to stay focused on the real reason I was out in the woods – to hike.

Rangeley, ME – 220.4 miles to Katahdin

A fun fact about Rangeley is that the town is located exactly halfway between the Equator and the North Pole! However, the trail was several miles south of Rangeley and to get into town, I needed a nine mile hitch. Luckily, people on the small backroads of Maine are very polite and I got a hitch into town with a fisherman from Rangeley. His wife sent him out to collect river stones for her, and when he opened the trunk of his sedan, I saw about ten milk crates full of polished stones. He dropped me off at the IGA just outside town and I went into the store to get my food. When I checked out, my jaw almost hit the floor when I saw the total price of all the food I bought. My two-and-a-half-day resupply cost me a whopping $90, which was ridiculous considering I typically got 4 or 5 days of food for that price. Needless to say, if I ever find myself in Rangeley again, I will not be stopping at that IGA!

Flabbergasted, I went outside and sat on a picnic table along the side of the store and ate my dinner. I was surprised over the last two days how well the Andover Mexican food sat in my stomach, but that all changed a few minutes later when I ventured back into the store to use their restroom…. That bathroom was probably uninhabitable for the next few days. Someone else waited for me to finish to use the bathroom, and as I walked towards the store entrance, I heard him yell "Oh my God!" from behind me. I grinned and strolled out of the store.

When I got back outside, I was joined by two other hikers, Potatoes and Kiwasabi. We were all headed back to the trail and to the same shelter that night. After finishing our dinner, the three of us walked over to the road and attempted to get a group hitchhike. Thankfully, a couple from Rhode Island just left IGA and saw us all standing out by the road and fit us all in their SUV and drove us back to the trail. Unfortunately, it was dark by the time we reached the trail, it was already dark and I had no choice but to continue on to the next shelter two miles ahead, so I put on my headlamp and began trekking out into the night with Coyote (another hiker...not an animal).

Stratton, ME – 188.2 miles to Katahdin

Before I reached Stratton, I was miserable. I spent the last two days (since Rangeley) in a constant 48-hour rainstorm, and I was both exhausted and drenched from head to foot. So it wasn't shocking when I decided to yellow blaze a portion of the trail after descending Sugarloaf Mountain. I quickly got a hitch from another section hiker from Pennsylvania, and she dropped me off at Stratton, a small town set at the crossroads of western Maine on the edge of Flagstaff Lake. Getting food was my first priority, so I went to the only store in town, Fotter's Market, and bought provisions for the next leg of the journey.

I decided to eat a late lunch on a bench outside the store. I bought a half-gallon of chocolate milk, four large crème horns, a quart of strawberry yogurt, and a large bag of potato chips for lunch. About ten minutes after I finished eating, my stomach turned over, which was either because of the massive quantity of food I ate or the fact that I just consumed more than 100 grams of saturated fat in one sitting. My face went ash white and I simultaneously felt like I was going to throw up and pass out, so I ran behind the store and laid face-down on the gravel parking lot. Someone must have seen me laying out there, because fifteen minutes later, someone came to see if I was okay, and I barely mustered enough strength to tell him I was okay. I kept still, and after another thirty minutes, the feeling started to pass away, enough so that I got up and walked down the street to the library.

I knew I had more paperwork to do for graduate school, so when I got an hour of time on a computer at the library, I got some forms filled in. There, I thought for the first time about life after the trail. After all, I was less than 200 miles from Katahdin and graduate school started in a month. I finished the work I needed to, just before the library closed for the day. Once it closed, I sat outside the doorway and charged my batteries until it started to sprinkle. I packed up my things and headed back in the soggy weather to get a hitch to the trail. Fifteen minutes later, I got a ride back to the trail, and I hiked into the Bigelows for the night.

Caratunk, ME – 151.2 miles to Katahdin

My story about Caratunk deserved a whole different section where I told the entire story, so to read that story, go to the section called "Krossing the Kennebec with Kim." The issue that hikers face is that the only way to get into Caratunk is by canoe, and there are only a few hours every day the canoe operator brings hikers across the Kennebec River. I arrived at the river too late, and to make a long story short, I got a ride from a local across the river in a stand-up paddleboard, in a thunderstorm. We made it across alive (spoiler alert), and I spent the night in her guest bedroom.

In the morning, I thanked Kim a thousand times and left to pick up my resupply package, which my parents put together and mailed to me. The post office in Caratunk had extremely limited hours, so hikers were encouraged to send and pick up packages from one of the businesses in town. I had mine sent to Caratunk House Bed and Breakfast, and when I arrived, I picked up my package and enjoyed one of their famous vanilla milkshakes. I ate it on the porch (and enjoyed being shaded from the misty rain) and headed out on my final ten or so days left on the trail.

Monson, ME – 114.5 miles to Katahdin

One of the most difficult sections of the trail was the Hundred Mile Wilderness, which is located just north of Monson. It isn't the most challenging terrain that hikers faced on the trail, but it is a big logistical challenge. This was the longest that hikers on the Appalachian Trail go between resupply points, and there is 100 miles to the nearest road and resupply (Abol Bridge Campground). I was focused on quantity when I reached Monson, and I knew I needed five- or six-days' worth of food to reach the other side. I learned a little bit of history about Monson as I walked into town. I passed huge slag piles along the side of the road along with giant ponds hewn out of the cliffs, which were filled with turquoise water. These turned out to be slate quarries, and I learned that Monson was famous for its slate, which was used for roofing and various other niches.

Once I got into town, I went straight to the Appalachian Trail Visitor Center, which was much more unofficial than I imagined. I thought I would be able to get a permit for Baxter Park there, but they couldn't help me out much except give me some information on trail conditions for the upcoming miles. I first resupplied at the Monson General Store, but I held back because the food was expensive. I went across the street to my next option, Pete's Place, and got more food, but they only had a very limited selection of food available.

Shaw's Hiker Hostel is perhaps the most well-known hostel on the entire Appalachian Trail, and since it is in Monson, I knew I needed to visit it when I was in town. I looked for Shaw and asked if their hiker store was open. He told me they closed ten minutes ago and wouldn't reopen for another two hours, which was annoying because I wanted to be back on the trail by then. With the disappointing news, I picked up my belongings and trudged back across town to the last place where I could find food, an Irving gas station. The selection I found there was better than I expected, and the food I needed was reasonably priced. I purchased all the food that I thought I needed to get through the Hundred Mile Wilderness, and I started walking back to the trail, which was a few miles north of the other side of town. After walking along the road until I got out of town, I started hitching for a ride, and a local named Charlie gave me a ride to the trailhead. And just like that, I finished visiting my last trail town.

Thru Hiker Lingo

Just as people from different parts of the United States have their own funky vernacular and words, the same can be said for hikers. We speak in lingo all the time, and this section is synonymous to a dictionary definition for many of the words that hikers use on the trail and I use in this book. Hopefully, after learning these words, you too can speak trail-ese!

Appalachian Trail (AT)
- A 2200-mile continuous footpath from **Springer Mountain** in Georgia to **Mount Katahdin** in Maine
- A once-in-a-lifetime opportunity to make indescribable memories and meet lifetime friends

ATC
- Appalachian Trail Conservancy
- The group that coordinates trail maintenance and alerts hikers to dangers on the trail

AYCE
- All-You-Can-Eat
- A place where hikers eat their money's worth in food

Baseweight
- The total weight of a hiker's pack, excluding food, water, and fuel
- A whopping 32 pounds on the **Appalachian Trail**, and subsequently lowered to 25 pounds for the **Pacific Crest Trail**

Bear Boxes

- Metal lockers located at some shelters to prevent bears from eating your food

Bear Canisters

- Plastic containers that are supposedly difficult for bears to break into to reach the food inside

Bear Hang

- The process of hanging your food bag from a tree
- Should be located 12 feet off ground, 6 feet from tree trunk, and 6 feet from branch it is on (which never happens)

Black Flies

- The most well-known species of biting flies found along the trail, especially in the Northeast

Blaze

- A 2" by 6" white rectangle painted on trees and rocks along the side of the trail that help hikers avoid getting lost

Blowdown

- A tree that fell onto the trail that partially or fully obstructs the trail

Blue Blazing

- Hiking a side trail on the **Appalachian Trail,** whether to see a vista, a refreshing **spring,** or to skip a portion of the trail

Boardwalk

- A type of walkway over a wet section of trail usually made of a log sawed in half that is extremely dangerous and slippery when wet

Bounce Box

- A box that hikers mail to themselves at different post offices so they can "bounce" items ahead to future towns when they need more supplies

Brain

- The upper part of a backpack where quick access items are stored
- A part of my body that clearly wasn't functioning properly since I decided to spend months alone in the wilderness

Bridle Path

- A trail that is (or was) used for pack animals or horses

Bushwhacking

- The painstaking process of crossing a section of woods without a trail, which often ends with the hiker being badly cut and bruised

Caretaker

- Someone who watches over a **shelter** or a mountain peak

Cat Hole

- A 6" to 8" deep hole dug into the ground to poop into

Cell Service

- One of the greatest things on the trail, which allows you to go shopping, check the weather, or talk to your loved ones

Civilization

- Anywhere but the **Appalachian Trail** (or **Pacific Crest Trail**)

Continental Divide Trail (CDT)

- A 3100-mile long trail that follows the Western Continental Divide from New Mexico to Glacier National Park in Montana

Convergence

- The time along the trail where **NOBO** and **SOBO** hikers pass each other

Cowboy Camping

- Sleeping in the backcountry without a tent or hammock, often on rocks at a peak
- An excellent way to catch **hypothermia** or get fined

DACS

- "Day After Civilization Syndrome"
- An unofficial mental health issue that occurs one day after hikers realize how life in **civilization** is and feel a desire to return to their normal lives (mainly for safety and food availability)

Day Hiker

- A hiker who is on the **Appalachian Trail** just for one or two days, similar to a weekender
- The most despised type of hiker in the eyes of a **thru hiker**
- Easily distinguished from long-distance hikers because they don't have a permanent stench

DEET

- N,N-diethyl-*m*-toluamide
- The active ingredient in insect repellants, considered by many to be toxic
- The only defense that hikers have against bloodthirsty swarms of **mosquitoes**

Dollar General

- According to many hikers, if this store is in town, then it is a true **trail town**
- A "dollar" store where most items are not $1

False Peak

- A peak that appears to be the mountain top, but upon reaching that location, it turns out the summit is higher
- A great way to dash the hopes of a hiker

Fire Tower

- Metal tower located at top of some mountains to assist with fire detection
- Allow hikers to get views on otherwise **wooded summits**

Flip-Flopper

- A hiker who hikes a large swath of the trail and then switches to another portion of the trail
- Example: A hiker who hikes from PA to ME, then from PA to GA

Ford

- A dangerous type of river crossing where hikers are expected to wade across a river with all their gear
- Are typically between shin- and knee-deep, but can be waist-deep
- Maine's version of a bridge

Gap
- The lowest point on a mountain ridge between two peaks
- Commonly found in Pennsylvania and southern New England

Giardia
- A parasitic disease that is caused by contacting contaminated food or water and causes diarrhea, fatigue, and cramps
- The reason you filter your water, regardless of how clean it looks

Gondola
- The building at the top of a ski lift

Gore-Tex
- According to any older hiker on the trail, the only company that has products that can keep yourself dry

Grade
- A value that describes the incline (steepness) of a trail
- Equivalent to about two times the angle of the slope (15° angle ≈ 30% grade)
- A letter earned in school that is somehow a measure of intelligence

Green Tunnel
- A trail that is covered by trees and other vegetation that impede most views
- A great description of the **Long Trail**

Hand Sanitizer
- The only personal hygiene item that can clean your hands

Hiker Box
- A box found at most businesses and **hostels** where hikers can deposit or pick up items that are shared with other hikers

Hiker Hunger
- A form of starvation that hikers develop after 2-3 weeks on the trail where they are so calorie-starved that they eat anything and everything they see

Hiker Midnight
- The time that most hikers go to sleep, generally about 9:00 PM

Hiker-friendly

- A person or business that welcomes stinky, sweaty hikers

Hitchhiking

- Sticking your thumb up to strange passersby in vehicles
- The art of coaxing a stranger to pull off to the side of the road and allow you to ride with them to the nearest town

Hostel

- A hotel for hikers that can't afford a hotel room
- A business along the trail that caters to hikers and allows them to stay the night for a fee or other service the hiker can provide

Hypothermia

- An extremely dangerous situation where a person's internal body temperature drops below 95°F, which can cause extreme confusion and death
- An affliction that can occur when hiking on a cold and rainy day (even in the middle of summer)

Ibuprofen

- A nonsteroidal anti-inflammatory drug used to reduce pain and swelling
- Commonly taken multiples times during the day, generally in the morning and around noon
- Consumption is generally proportional to the trail difficulty

Katahdin

- The northern terminus of the Appalachian Trail
- Infamous as the most difficult mountain on the entire trail
- A wake-up call for SOBO hikers and just another day on the trail for NOBOs

Knorr's Sides

- Uncooked packages of rice and pasta that are commonly eaten by hikers for dinner who pour boiling water into the package and let it cook for ten minutes

Krummholz

- Vegetation that is badly misshapen or deformed due to extreme weather conditions found near **tree line**

LASHer

- "Long-Ass Section Hiker"
- A more glorified title than a **section hiker**
- People who cannot devote a whole year to hiking the trail due to school, weather, and other commitments

Lean-to

- A type of structure found along the **Appalachian Trail** with three walls and a roof, similar to a **shelter**

Long Trail

- A trail that isn't extremely "long" by AT standards, at only 272 miles in length
- A rugged trail through the Green Mountains across the backbone of Vermont from the Massachusetts border to the Canadian border

Loon

- An aquatic bird found along the trail in Maine with a distinct red eye and a unique bird call

Lyme Disease

- A tick-borne disease commonly identified by a bullseye on the skin and may be treated with antibiotics

Maildrop

- **Resupplying** using a package that was mailed to you on the trail

McDonalds

- A fast food restaurant that accepts hikers and [generally] allows hikers to refill their drink multiple times
- Considered by some to be a staple of a true **trail town**

Mosquitoes

- Winged insects that are extremely prevalent near bodies of water and make life miserable for everyone
- One species that thrives along the entire trail because of hikers

Nero

- A day when a hiker walks nearly zero miles on the **Appalachian Trail**
- A good way to rest your body and not feel bad about taking a **zero**

Night Hiking

- Hiking at night, preferentially during a full moon

NOBO

- Hiking northbound on the **Appalachian Trail** (Georgia → Maine)

Notch

- An abrupt and steep-sloped point in a mountain range between two peaks
- Common in the White Mountains and southern Maine

Pacific Crest Trail (PCT)

- A 2650-mile hiking and equestrian trail stretching from the Mexican border at Campo, California to the Canadian Border near Manning Provincial Park, British Columbia
- A much more remote and isolated trail than the **Appalachian Trail**
- A difficult trail to hike due to varied terrain and extreme weather

Palisades Parkway

- The only road crossing on the trail where hikers emerge from the woods and are forced to cross a divided highway with cars passing them driving 70 mph

Pass

- A navigable route through a series of ridges or mountains at a natural low point

Permethrin

- An insecticide applied to clothing that kills **mosquitoes**, biting flies, ticks, and chiggers

Piped Spring

- A **spring** fitted with a pipe erected from the ground to prevent trampling the water source

Posthole

- The process of making footprints in the **snow** on the trail, generally as the first hiker to pass an area

Privy

- A shack in the middle of the woods where human waste is collected and converted into soil for the forest floor
- The closest thing to a toilet on the **Appalachian Trail**

Purist

- A **thru hiker** on the **Appalachian Trail** that hikes the entire distance, insisting on passing every single white blaze
- Referred to as the "Grammar Nazis of Hiking"

Radar

- A digital meteorological map displaying the location and movement of various precipitation-producing storms

Rain

- A form of liquid dihydrogen monoxide that falls from the sky, particularly heavy and for days at a time in Maine

Rainfly

- The upper part of a tent that is intended to prevent rain from entering the tent

Resupply

- The process of obtaining necessary supplies (usually food) to continue a long-distance hike
- Usually completed every 3-5 days

REI

- Recreation Equipment Inc.
- A great place to get advice and gear for hikers of any and all skill levels

Road Walk

- To walk along the side of the road, either to **yellow blaze** or to walk into town

Rock Hop
- The process of stepping or jumping from rock to rock across a stream

Sawyer Squeeze
- A type of handheld water filter that filters out viruses and bacteria from water

Section Hiker
- A hiker who walks sections of the AT, spanning from only a few days to about a month on the trail
- Spends less time on the trail than a **LASHer**

Shakedown
- An item-by-item inspection of all hiking gear in a pack to determine if the need for an item is worth its weight, usually occurring about 100 miles into a hike

Shelter
- A structure found every 8-15 miles along the **Appalachian Trail** where hikers can spend the night with a roof over their head

Slackpacking
- A form of hiking where a hiker stays at a **hostel** and leaves all their overnight gear there, rides to the trailhead in the morning, hikes for 10-25 miles stretch with a much lighter pack, and then spends another night at the **hostel** and continues on with a regular pack
- A form of cheating that is viewed negatively by **purists** and most AT hikers

Snow
- The solid and air-rich form of dihydrogen monoxide that falls from the sky when the air temperature is below freezing

SOBO
- Hiking southbound on the **Appalachian Trail** (Maine → Georgia)

Spring
- The point at which water emerges from an underground aquifer
- The main source of water for all hikers

Springer Mountain

- The southern terminus to the **Appalachian Trail**
- The most common mountain that **NOBO**s quit the **Appalachian Trail** on each year

Stealth Camping

- The act of secretly camping on the side of the trail at an undeveloped site and leaving early the next morning to avoid being caught

Switchback

- A series of curves along a trail that allows hikers to ascend a mountain at a much lower **grade** compared to going straight up
- A trail feature that is absent in much of the Northeast on the AT

Tailings

- A pile of slag or debris that is residuum from a mining operation

Thru Hiker

- A hiker that consecutively walks the entire distance of the **Appalachian Trail** in one year
- Easily recognized due to rugged appearance, filthy gear, and a unique character trait

Trail Angel

- Someone who provides **trail magic**

Trail Family

- A group of hikers who band together to hike part or all the **Appalachian Trail**

Trail Guide

- A paperback or electronic guide that assists hikers through various waypoints along the trail

Trail Legs

- A physical state where your lower-body muscles have significantly strengthened, allowing you to hike much faster
- Typically develop after 2 or 3 weeks on the trail

Trail Magic

- Any sort of help that hikers get from strangers who provide them with food, beverages, or words of encouragement

Trail Names

- Sacred names that hikers earn, usually due to a personal folly or intriguing characteristic

Trail Register

- Lists along the trail at various points of interest and at all **shelters** where hikers register they were there and provide anecdotes for other hikers

Trail Town

- A town along or near the **Appalachian Trail** that has **hiker-friendly** businesses

Tree Line

- The elevation at which trees cannot grow, which varies considerably by mountain and latitude
- The point that you want to be below when thunderstorm approaches

Triple Crown

- A hiker who has successfully completed the **Appalachian Trail**, **Pacific Crest Trail**, and **Continental Divide Trail**

Ultralight Hiking

- A form of hiking where the hiker's **baseweight** is less than 10 pounds
- A great way to experience **hypothermia** and starvation

Virgin Forest

- An area of forest that has not been disturbed by human presence and are remnants of the vast ancient forests of North America
- Found along the AT in Sages Ravine, CT and Elephant Mountain, ME

Walmart

- A place where long-distance hikers actually fit in with normal shoppers

White Blazing

- Hiking on the Appalachian Trail and passing white blazes

Widowmaker

- A tree or branch that precariously balanced over a campsite and could potentially fall and kill a hiker camping below

Wifi

- One of the most basic human needs in towns along the **Appalachian Trail**
- An opportunity to browse the web, talk with others, or post pictures of your hike without using cellular data

Wooded Summit

- The type of summit that infuriates all hikers after hiking uphill for hours only to see more trees and no view

Work for Stay (WFS)

- A system in the White Mountains where **thru hikers** can perform various tasks to assist **caretakers** and be rewarded by gorging on food and sleeping on the floor of a hut

Yellow Blazing

- A person on the **Appalachian Trail** that **road walks** a section instead of hiking on the actual trail

Yo-Yo

- A person who starts hiking the **Appalachian Trail** in Georgia and hikes to **Katahdin** in Maine, then turns around and hikes back to Georgia in the same year

Yogi

- A special trait of some hikers that can allow them to be fed like wild animals from humans who feel bad about the hikers' state

Zero

- The most magical days on the trail for your body but the least productive days on the trail
- Occurs when a hiker decides to hike a whopping 0 miles in a day, usually done in a trail town due to food availability

Made in the USA
Middletown, DE
30 January 2020